John Naish

Put WHAT WHERE?

OVER 2000 YEARS OF BIZARRE SEX ADVICE

HARPER
element

Also by John Naish

The Hypochondriac's Handbook

Happiness is the true test. Never mind what books – including this one – say you should do. If you are happy, and your partner is too, leave well enough alone.

Eustace Chesser, *Love Without Fear* (1940)

HarperElement
An Imprint of HarperCollins*Publishers*
77–85 Fulham Palace Road,
Hammersmith, London W6 8JB

The website address is: www.thorsonselement.com

and *HarperElement* are trademarks of
HarperCollins*Publishers* Ltd

First published by HarperElement 2005

1 3 5 7 9 10 8 6 4 2

A catalogue record of this book
is available from the British Library

ISBN 0 00 721423 5

Printed and bound in Great Britain by
Clays Ltd, St Ives plc

CONTENTS

PREFACE

This book is both a history of sex advice and a treasury of bizarre suggestions from throughout the ages. It is organized like a club sandwich. The historical chapters cover this strange world in chronological order, from 200 BC to the 1970s, and are interlayered with the cream of humankind's oddest sex-advice quotes. These are grouped by topic and take you, stage-by-stage, through the whole gamut of love-making, from finding a partner through to sex, fetishes, afterplay and unfaithfulness. If you learn nothing else, please remember: never bite your partner's eyeballs.

One

INTRODUCTION

Mating. Reproduction. The survival of the species. How much more crucial does it get?

You'd think *homo sapiens* would have sorted out that one pretty sharpish. But no. Since the start of civilization, human sex has been absurdly complicated by a steady dripfeed of self-appointed experts: moralists, pundits, visionaries, ju-ju men, zealots and learned academics – all claiming to know the magical secrets of lovemaking. And they were all prepared to sell their wisdom to you at a very reasonable price. Just as every generation likes to think it invented sexual intercourse, we also like to think we invented sex advice, or at least built it on a very limited number of predecessors: the *Kama Sutra*, maybe Marie Stopes' 1918 *Married Love* and the 1970s *The Joy of Sex*. But in fact today's maelstrom of lovemaking manuals, videos and DVDs has a far richer and more twisted heritage than that. The genre is way older than the novel, and takes us right back to an ancient Chinese tomb-hoard of books first written in 300 BC.

Every era has had its Dr Ruths dictating to us the correct way, the right place, the essential time, the appropriate shape, the perfect partner and, of course, the ultimate naughtiness. And what a proud parade: they feature, to mention but a few, Roman poets, medieval woman-haters, Victorian adventurers, astral travellers, gay sandal-makers, dope peddlers, racial-purity fanatics, wholewheat snack-makers, an impotent love guru, a divorced virgin and a toga-wearing erectophobe. If these self-appointed sexperts share one common characteristic, it's a special strain of eccentricity. Along with the throng of plain charlatans came the freaks, geeks, dreamers, anarchists, rebels and lost souls who were so out of kilter with society that they felt driven to preach about a legally perilous subject in a manner almost guaranteed to offend those in authority, scandalize friends and families, and frequently land them behind bars.

One of their great motives was, as usual, power – the power to tell people what they should and should not do in their most private moments. But they were also driven by a streak of evangelism, the messianic eye-gleam of people convinced that they had found the sexual solution to life's miseries. In many ways, the old advice books were not actually about sex itself, but alchemy: promising to reveal secret formulae for the perfect existence, the greatest happiness, and to open up a conduit to divine wisdom. Some even claimed that secret bouts of ritualistic congress could grant you magical powers and immortality.

Despite (or because of) this legion of advisors, sensible sex advice was a long time coming. It was only very recently that we finally learnt the precise mechanics of reproduction. This information gap didn't stop the experts, though. They simply made it all up, using as their guide a hodge-podge of previous books, current fashion, a bit of fieldwork and their own deep personal prejudices. But if old sex books can't help us much with the art and science of lovemaking, they do open for us a new window on to history's lurid mosaic of obsession, fear, lust, hatred, fantasy and insanity. Welcome to the human condition.

So much for the writers, but what about us, the readers? Why do we spend precious money and time on sex manuals? Bonobo monkeys are our closest primate cousins, and although you wouldn't catch a bonobo monkey with his nose stuck in a mating manual, they enjoy a sexual repertoire – multipositions, group sex, lesbianism, etc. – that is at least as complex, acrobatic and experimental as most human couples ever sample. True, bonobos have sex in public, which humans mostly don't – so their young get an education that consists of 'watch it, learn it and try it'. Then again, the human imagination, and the ample amount of time it dedicates to sexual fantasy, can generally be trusted to work out all the physical permutations on its own. But there is something else about the private nature of human sex: it plants nagging questions in people's heads – am I normal; am I doing it in a way that is correct, fun, efficient and legal; and, of course, can I do it better?

Education aside, one can't ignore the titillation factor associated with anything to do with sex, particularly in decades past when such information was heavily censored and even the most straightforward information could be considered hot stuff – although much of it came across as a mix between an engineering treatise, a lengthy sermon and a wholefood cookbook. That sort of illicit thrill scores bulls-eye on the brain's reward centre – which responds by sending the message, 'That was good, let's do it again, it might be better next time'. Thus, sex manuals throughout history have elbowed hot cakes into second place on the sales charts. The books have frequently used the same sales lure – there's an amazing secret regime revealed inside that will truly change your life. Today the same trick is used to sell diet, exercise and psychological self-help books. The song remains the same: our modern era is remarkable only in the sheer, overwhelming volume of sex advice being churned out and avidly consumed. One in four British women says they own a sex manual, according to a survey by the publishers Dorling Kindersley in 2003. Writers and publishers are putting out new sex books every month. Everyone is at it, from former porn stars to the car-workshop manual maker Haynes. Then there are DVDs, videos, websites and mass advertising – the *Sunday Telegraph* carries adverts for a 'clitoral stimulator' and none of its readers' horses bolt.

We've become saturated with sex advice. That should, in theory, make for bookshelves crowded with surprising, amazing and revelatory material. In reality, though, it doesn't. Now that medicine has

sorted out the science and most of us share a liberal
sense of morality, the texts all tend to say rather
the same thing, albeit in a variety of permutations.
Ho hum. That's why, if you still fancy a spot of true
variety and spice between the covers of a sex
manual, there's only one place to go – back in time,
to where all the strange folk and their peculiar practices lie quietly waiting for you. Just one word of
warning, though: please don't try any of it at home.

Caution! Before You Start Sex, Remember . . .

Tight buns and corsets cause nymphomania

Dr John Cowan, *The Science of a New Life* (1888)

The constricting of the waist and abdomen by corsets, girdles and waistbands prevents the return of venous blood to the heart, and the consequent overloading of the sexual organs causes the unnatural excitement of the sexual system.

The majority of women, adoring followers of the goddess Fashion, wear their hair in a large, heavy knot on the back part of the head, and when their own is insufficient to make a roll enough, false hair is added. This great pressure on the small brain produces great heat in the part and causes an unusual flow of the blood to the area of amativeness and, if persisted in, a chronic inflammation of the sexual organ, and a chronic desire for its sexual exercise … It is almost impossible that she should lead other than a life of sexual excess.

Sexual jealousy can ruin your skin

Fang Nei Chi (Records of the Bedchamber),
Sui Dynasty (AD 590–618)

A woman should not allow herself to become jealous or sad if she sees her man copulate with another woman, for then her yin essence will become over-excited. She will be afflicted by pains while sitting and standing, and the vaginal emissions will flow spontaneously. These are ills that will cause a woman to wither and age before her time. Therefore she should guard against this.

Never share a bedroom

Marie Stopes, *Married Love* (1918)

It may enchant a man once – perhaps even twice – to watch his goddess screw her hair up into a tight and unbecoming knot and soap her ears. But it is inherently too unlovely a proceeding to retain indefinite enchantment ... So far as is possible ensure that you allow your husband to come upon you only when there is delight in the meeting. Whenever the finances allow, the husband and wife should have separate bedrooms, failing that they should have a curtain which can at will be drawn so as to divide the room they share. No soul can grow to its full nature without its spells of solitude. A woman's body and soul should be essentially her own, and that can only be so if she has an inviolable retreat.

Ejaculating may repel your partner

Theodoor Hendrik Van de Velde, *Ideal Marriage,
Its Physiology and Technique* (1928)

After mental and emotional excitement the smell of
the semen is more acrid, after muscular exertion,
more aromatic and, after several repeated acts of
coitus in rapid succession it becomes fainter, but
stale and unpleasant.

I know of one highly talented and delicately sensitive woman who abruptly terminated a liaison on
finding, at the first act of sexual intercourse, that the
special seminal odour of the man was intolerably
unpleasant to her ... It may be said in general that the
odour of semen is exciting and stimulating to women
and unpleasant, even nauseating to men. For a
woman, the odour of the beloved man's semen is
delightful and excites her anew; but that of an
unloved mate fills her with loathing.

Never make love with goblins

Fang Nei Chi (Records of the Bedchamber),
Sui Dynasty (AD 590–618)

If a person has an unbalanced sex life, his sexual
desire will increase. Devils and goblins will take
advantage of this condition. They assume human
shape and have sexual intercourse with such a
person. They are much more skilled in this art than
human beings, so much so that their victim becomes
completely enamoured of the ghostly lover. Those

people will keep the relation secret and will not speak about its delights. In the end they succumb alone, without anyone being the wiser.

The after-effects of copulation with an incubus can be cured by the following method: the man should copulate all day and night without ejaculating, then after seven days the disease will be cured. When his body is so fatigued that he cannot continue the act, the man should let his penis rest in the woman's vagina and he will benefit all the same. If this disease is not treated as indicated here, the victim will die in a few years.

If one wishes a proof of the existence of incubi, one has but to repair alone to a marsh place far away in the mountains, in spring or autumn. One should stay there in a condition of complete tranquillity, staring into space and concentrating one's thoughts on sexual intercourse. After three days and three nights, the body will suddenly become alternately cold and hot, the heart will be troubled and the vision blurred.

Then, a man engaging in this experiment will meet a woman, and a woman a man. During sexual intercourse with such an incubus one will experience a pleasure that is greater than ever felt while copulating with an ordinary human being. But at the same time one will become subject to this disease which is difficult to cure.

Evil women can contain iron

Albertus Magnus, *De Secretis Mulierum*
(*The Secrets of Women*) (c. 1478)

O my companions you should be aware that although
certain women do not know the secret cause of what
I shall describe, many women are familiar with the
effect, and many evils result from this. For when men
have sexual intercourse with these women it sometimes happens that they suffer a large wound and a
serious infection of the penis because of iron that
has been placed in the vagina, for some women or
harlots are instructed in this and other ill deeds.

Post-climax calamities

Havelock Ellis, *Psychology of Sex: a manual for students* (1933)

So profound is the organic convulsion involved by the process of detumescence that serious effects have sometimes followed coitus. Especially in men, not only death itself, but numerous disorders and accidents have been known to follow immediately after coitus, these results being mainly due to the vascular and muscular excitement involved by the process of detumescence.

Fainting, vomiting, involuntary urination and defecation have been noted as occurring in young men after first coitus. Epilepsy has been not infrequently recorded. Lesions of various organs, even rupture of the spleen, have sometimes taken place.

In men of mature age the arteries have at times been unable to resist the high blood pressure and cerebral haemorrhage with paralysis has occurred. In elderly men the excitement of intercourse with young wives or with prostitutes has sometimes caused death. Such results are, however, exceptional. They tend to occur in persons who are abnormally sensitive or who have imprudently transgressed the obvious rules of sexual hygiene.

Sex during the monthlies causes ...

The Treasury of Natural Secrets
(anon., Italy, 16th century)

Physical weakness
Ten years' premature ageing
Simple-mindedness
Loss of libido
Aches and pains in stomach, feet, eyes, brain,
    head
Ringing in ears
High fevers
Tremors
Weak nerves
Poor eyesight
Baldness
Backaches
Kidney and bladder pains
Bad breath
Foul body odour

Just put the Hoover down

Dr Alex Comfort, *The Joy of Sex* (1972)

Never fool around sexually with a vacuum cleaner.

Two

MANKIND'S FIRST MANUALS

In archaeology, as in life, if you want to find sex books, look in the son's room.

The first lovemaking guides in human history may well be in the form of 4,000-year-old cave paintings found in countries such as France, Peru and Japan, showing women or couples in various positions, naked or wearing strange headgear. But without any words to accompany the pictures, we simply don't know: they could have been educational, religious or ceremonial, or simply prototypes of readers' wives. The earliest actual written sex books we have were only discovered in 1973. They date from around 2,400 years ago and were hidden in a Chinese family tomb, in the section where the son was interred. The books were greatest-hits compilations of Chinese wisdom that had already been around for a century. The questions they raised have proved extremely persistent – if you read a modern sex manual, glossy magazine or newspaper advice column, they will still be there.

If the advice these ancient books contain were written in the form of modern magazine coverlines, it would read:

FOUR SEASONS OF SEX:
AND WHY AUTUMN IS HOT, HOT, HOT

Your 100 thrusts to happiness
Wild new positions: tiger roving, gibbon
grabbing ... and fish gobbling
Sexplanation: read your partner's writhing
From your wrists to your peaks – the ultimate
in-the-mood massage
Aphrodisiacs to keep you up all night!
And
Exclusive: your love route to immortality

The manuscripts were among a treasure-house
of ancient books discovered in Mawangdui Tomb
Three, in the city of Changsha in the Hunan
province of China. The tomb was a horseshoe-
shaped mound of earth about 30ft high and 90ft in
diameter that contained the bodies and possessions
of the Hou Family. It took two years, from 1972
to 1974, to excavate the 2,100-year-old Han-period
tombs, which contained more than 3,000 cultural
relics and a complete female corpse. In among 28
silk books were seven medical manuscripts, which
together constitute mankind's first *Joy of Sex*.

The tomb's occupants, Dai Marquis Licang, his
wife and son, were part of the local political elite.
Licang was the King of Changsha's prime minister
for seven years from 193 BC. Each body lay in its own
tomb, inside a set of coffins stacked like Russian
dolls, one inside another. The Number Three Tomb –

the book room – is now restored to its original state. The son was called Li, and his skeleton indicates that he was about 30 when he died in 168 BC, though most of the medical manuscripts seem to have been copied in 200 BC. References in them indicate they are from earlier texts that must have circulated around 300 BC.

Li was an avid book collector whose hobby covered several specialist fields, including medicine. He would have been a whizz on *Mastermind*. We can only guess why his extensive library was buried alongside him: perhaps it was thought to have magical powers, or maybe the books were simply there to show his new pals in the afterlife what a wise and wealthy guy he'd been. The sex books were written on silk or on strips of wood or bamboo, and were found on top of a pile of silk manuscripts stored in the side compartment of a lacquer box.

Two of the texts focus on the bizarre mystical practice of 'sexual cultivation', which promises that if a man spends years having intercourse with hundreds of women (preferably virgins) without ejaculating, he will have received so much yin energy from female orgasms, and conserved so much of his male yang energy by not orgasming, that he will become immortal (either that, or his testes would explode). The idea was attributed to Ancestor Peng, who is said to have died at the age of 300, some time around 4 BC and 3 BC, thanks to his strict 'way of hygiene' which covered personal cleanliness, diet and sex. Ejaculating frequently, the books warn, wears a man out, because semen is full of the life-force, chi.

A man could preserve his penis chi either by not climaxing, or by climaxing but preventing ejaculation. Medical experts suggest this can be done by applying hand pressure to a point between the scrotum and the anus, which blocks the urethra. Peng's theory was that the semen would be diverted up the spine into the brain. In fact, if you block your urethral tube behind your scrotum, the sperm is squirted into your bladder and gets urinated out. This whole idea might seem insane, but it has resurfaced in different forms for centuries. It reappeared in Chinese books printed in 1066, 1307 and 1544, and was later published in Japan. It also crops up in different cultures around the globe at different times. It even became popular, as we will see, in nineteenth-century America.

The Mawangdui guides do not only cover non-ejaculation. There is an entire regime dictating when to have sex: in spring you can do it from evening until after midnight; in summer from evening until midnight; in winter from evening until around 11pm; and in autumn, hooray, whenever you like – though the text then says that men should never try having intercourse in the morning.

The books also tell you in confusing and often tedious detail the precise operation of lovemaking, with a guide to foreplay using slow, sexual massage, the 'ideal 100-thrusts', and then the 'ten refinements' – which basically involve going up, down and from side to side, and changing your speed and depth – information that must surely have been old hat even 300 years before the birth of Christ. And with around 21 centuries to go before the invention of Viagra, the manuscripts offer their own aphrodisiac ideas, involving such exotic stimulant ingredients as swarming beetle larvae, wasps and dried snails.

The ancient Chinese also brought us the first sex-advice Q&As. The format so beloved of *Cosmopolitan* and co was created by books in which the legendary Yellow Emperor asked 'your common questions' of a team of expert female advisors with names such as the Plain Girl and the Mystery Girl, as well as (of course) a qualified doctor. The Yellow Emperor texts were frequently illustrated with pictures of sexual positions, and given to brides as part of their trousseau.

Despite its general uselessness, much of this advice remained in circulation in one form or another in China until the sixteenth century, when it was suppressed by the new regime of Confucianist emperors. They found all this sex stuff generally unspeakable and censored it so efficiently that subsequent Chinese writers never knew that it had even existed.

When to Have Sex

Never after a meal

Perfumed Garden of Sheik Nefzaoui (16th century),
translated into English by Sir Richard F. Burton

If you wish for sex, you should not have your stomach loaded with food and drink. If your stomach is full, only harm can come of it to both of you; you will have symptoms of apoplexy and gout, and the least evil that will be the consequence of it will be the inability of passing your urine, or weakness of sight.

And not before lunch

Ancestor Peng, in the introduction to *Yinshu*
(*The Pulling Book*), *c.* 186 BC

Morning is not the recommended time for men to practise sex.

18

Daytime - all day

R.T. Trall, *Sexual Physiology: a scientific and popular exposition of the fundamental problems in sociology* (1867)

If children are to be begotten ... the sexual embrace should be had in the light of day. It is only then that the magnetic forces and the nervous system are in their highest condition of functional activity and the body, refreshed by sleep, is in its most vigorous condition. But it should not be the hurried act of the early morning, like a hasty meal before a day's work ... Surely, if sexual intercourse is worth doing at all, it is worth doing well. And it would not exalt its importance one iota above its real merits if certain days were set apart, consecrated, to the conjugal embrace. It might be one day in seven, or one day in twenty, or more or less.

Seasonal sex

Giovanni Marinello, *Medicine Pertinent to the Infirmities of Women* (Italy, 1563)

Least harmful: spring and winter
Use sparingly: summer
Use even more sparingly: autumn

Spring for men, autumn for women

Nicholas Venette, *The Mysteries of Conjugal Love Reveald* (1703)

Men are most apt for the company of women in winter and in spring; women most desirous of commerce with man in summer and autumn; and this proceeds from the contrary complexion, in respect both to the times and persons, which complexion is nothing else than the different mixtures of warmth with cold, and moisture with dryness ...

In my opinion, copulation is more seasonable in spring and winter; it may be used in the time of autumn, but in the heads of summer it should be carefully avoided, when the ordinary discharges of the body are so great ...

We ought to embrace when our belly is moderately filled, for at such a junction we feel a strange desire to be meddling.

Check the zodiac, and never after war ...

Ananga Ranga of Kalyanamalla (Stage of the Love God),
by the Indian poet Kalyan Mall (16th century)

Hot weather
Cold weather
Any time, in fact that's not springtime or the
    rains
Daytime – unless it's your woman's favourite
    time
When ill with fever
When tired from travel
When observing a religious rite
At the new moon
When the sun or a planet passes from one side
    of the zodiac to another
In the evening
When tired from warfare

Geddinthere! (Times she might be in the mood)

Koka Shastra (The Scripture of Koka),
by the Indian poet Kokkoka (12th century)

When tired from travel
Convalescing from a fever
Weary from dancing
The sixth month of pregnancy
A month after giving birth

Etiquette: when to introduce a new mistress to your wives

Chinese householder's notebook
(c. 16th century)

Recently I heard about a certain official who took unto him a new concubine. He locked himself in with her behind double doors and did not appear for three days. All his wives and concubines were highly incensed at this behaviour. This is indeed the wrong way.

The right method is for the man to control his desire and, for the time being not approaching the newcomer, concentrate his attention on the others. Every time he has sexual intercourse with his other women, he should make the newcomer stand at attention by the side of the ivory couch. Then, after four or five nights of this, he may for the first time copulate with the newcomer, but only with his principal wife and the other concubines present. This is the fundamental principle of harmony and happiness in one's women's quarters.

Three

CLASSICAL GAFFES

Owning a sex manual was not something you would shout about in ancient Greece: it was considered a sin against moderation, the primary virtue of the ancient world, and linked by critics to other faux pas such as gluttony, drunkenness and using prostitutes.

Greek writers of sex manuals were treated like the tabloid journalists of the day and labelled with the snappy title of *anaiskhuntographo* – 'writers of shameless things'.

This did not deter aspiring sex advisors from putting pen to papyrus, though, and writing love guides became a feminine speciality. An AD 10 lexicon claims that the first Greek to have published a sex manual was Astyanassa, whose official job title was Helen of Troy's 'body servant'. She is credited with being both the first person to discover all the workable positions for intercourse and the first to write them down. She was followed by Elephantis and Philaenis. Elephantis, the prostitute-poetess, is supposed to have detailed nine different postures. The Emperor Tiberius is said to have been an avid reader, but tantalizingly, although these postures are often mentioned in classical texts, they remain lost somewhere beneath the mattress of time.

The other leading writer, Philaenis, is also believed to have been a woman (though it might possibly have been a man pretending, in order to boost sales). Only a few fragments from a papyrus of hers, from 2 BC, survive. In her preamble, she claims to have written it all from her own experience, as an objective and scientific guide. On flattery, she recommends, 'Tell an older woman that she looks young. Tell an ugly woman that she looks "fascinating". Pick the woman's worst feature and then make it appear desirable.' Other writers who appear to have flourished at the time include Paxamus, a general hack who wrote the *Dodecatechnon*, a book of twelve erotic postures – which is once again sadly lost.

We have more luck with the Romans, particularly the celebrated writer Lucretius, who at around 50 BC seems to have stumbled on the 'Love Hurts' idea so beloved of pop songs. The fourth section of his *On the Nature of the Universe*, dedicated to sex and sensation, warns readers that they must dodge Cupid's darts: 'The wounded normally fall in the direction of their wound: the blood spurts out towards the source of the blow. So, when a man is pierced by the shafts of Venus, whether they are launched by a lad with womanish limbs or a woman radiating love from her whole body, he strives towards the source of the wound and craves to ejaculate the fluid drawn from out of his body into that

body. His speechless yearning foretells his pleasure.'
Messy.

Lucretius recommends that you try your best to
avoid all this. His solution is to evade true love by
embarking on a promiscuous sex spree: 'If you find
yourself thus passionately enamoured with someone,
you should keep well away from images that remind
you of them. Thrust from you anything that might
feed your passion, and turn your mind elsewhere.
Ejaculate the build-up of seed promiscuously and do
not hold on to it – by clinging to it you assure yourself
the certainty of heartsickness and pain ... Do not
think that by avoiding romantic love you are missing
the delights of sex. No, you are reaping the sort of
profits that carry with them no penalty.'

The Roman period also brought us the first example of a sex-manual martyr. Poor old Ovid (aka
Publius Ovidius Naso) is only the first of a long line
of authors whose sullied reputations, trashed
careers and broken lives litter the pages of this
book. He got himself banished to a far fringe of
empire for writing a bawdy guide to sexual postures,
the *Ars amatoria* (*The Art of Love*), which is a lads'-
mag treasury of tips on grooming, sex and seducing
your friends' wives.

Ovid was born in 43 BC in Sulmo – modern-day
Sulmona in central Italy – and studied in Athens
before moving to Rome where he dutifully worked
his way up to a decent civil service job. He then
decided on a radical career move into the world of
art and became a full-time poet. The gamble paid
off handsomely and his writing and wit soon won

him imperial fame and fortune. But at the age of 40 he made a rather less popular move, by treating his Roman readers to a pornographic poem. The *Ars amatoria* begins innocently enough: 'If anyone among this people know not the art of loving let him read my poem and having read be skilled in love. By skill, swift ships are sailed and rowed, by skill nimble chariots are driven: by skill must love be guided.' But its long closing passage was particularly risqué, suggesting sex-position tips for women that would show off their best parts (viz, if you've long legs, put them on your partner's shoulders; if you're saggy from childbirth, let him take you from behind; if you're short, go on top, and so on).

The verses mortally offended the somewhat strait-laced Emperor Augustus. The poem, along with another, undisclosed error, got him banished to the freezing cold, primitive town of Tomis on the Black Sea. (He cryptically wrote, 'two crimes, a poem and a blunder have brought me to ruin. I must keep silent.') He continued writing poetry and begging to be allowed home, but to no avail. Ovid died in exile eight years later, in AD 17. The persecution of his saucy poem did not, however, stop there. All Ovid's works were burned as obscene by the Dominican reformist preacher Girolamo Savonarola, in Florence in 1497 (though Savonarola met the same fiery fate himself a year later, after he upset the Vatican). And as late as 1928, an English translation of *Ars amatoria* was banned from America by US Customs.

The authorities might well remain reluctant to allow one of the late classical world's other guides on lovemaking to be published. The *Affairs of the Heart* is effectively the inner monologue of a bi-curious male. Written by Lucien (or very possibly someone doing a rough imitation of his work) around AD 4, it records the disputes between a straight philanderer and a gay pederast over whose sex life is more honest and pleasurable. The straight guy wins, and the text recommends that male readers should choose wives over young boys – not least because they last longer: a woman is desirable from maidenhood to middle age, whereas boys pass their prime as soon as their beard starts to grow. What's more, it adds, a woman can be used sexually just like a boy, thus offering 'two roads to pleasure'. Bonus, eh?

Where to Do It

Outdoors

Marie Stopes, *Married Love* (1918)

There are some who do realize the sacredness and the value of nature and sunlight. There must be many beautiful children who were conceived from unions which took place under natural conditions of nature and sunlight.

But beware cops and other vermin

Dr Alex Comfort, *The Joy of Sex* (1972)

Outdoor locations in wild areas are often flawed by vermin, ranging from ants and mosquitoes to rattle-snakes and officious cops.

And certainly not in these places

Ananga Ranga of Kalyanamalla (Stage of the Love God),
by the Indian poet Kalyan Mall (16th century)

In the presence of a holy man, a respectable
    old person or a great man
By rivers or streams
Next to wells or water tanks
Temples
Forts or castles
Guard-rooms, police stations, or other
    government places where prisoners are held
On a highway
In someone else's house
Forests, meadows or uplands
Cemeteries

The consequences of carnal connection at such places are disastrous. They breed misfortunes. If children are begotten, they turn out bad and malicious.

Low light, on top of the blankets

Rennie MacAndrew, *Life Long Love:*
healthy sex and marriage (1928)

Intimacy should always take place on top of the bed rather than beneath the blankets, so that each can enjoy seeing the physical charms of the other. Exhibitionism is not a perversion as a prologue to the consummation of love. Ideally, intercourse should be performed in a dimly lighted room, certainly not in the dark.

Four

NO SEX PLEASE, WE'RE MEDIEVAL ENGLISH

In the unenlightened Britain of the Middle Ages, the Church was hard at work cementing the foundations for centuries of sexual double-standards and miserabilism.

Its moral leaders could not actually ban sex – they had to be practical, and intercourse was the only reliable way that mere mortals could fulfil God's command to go forth and multiply. Nevertheless, the clergy shared St Paul and St Augustine's wholehearted distaste for this undignified and bestial act – especially if anyone appeared to be having fun while performing it. Lust was a tool of the serpent of Satan, which turned the natural and sinless act of marital baby-making into something damnably hellish. Enjoying marital sex (rather than only putting up with it) constituted a venial sin. Adultery or fornication, moreover, constituted a mortal sin. Celibacy was the safest recommended route to heaven.

So when the local peasants sought advice on the physical side of marriage, the clergy were less than encouraging. One of the Church's authoritative sources of sex do's and don'ts consisted of an

31

obsessively detailed inventory of acts that was apparently compiled by St Theodore of Tarsus, the Archbishop of Canterbury, from AD 668 to 690. In fact *The Penitential of Theodore* didn't contain any do's – they were all don'ts. The banned list included everything from receiving oral sex and masturbation, to bestiality and simply enjoying a cuddle with your spouse on holy days. Each offence was accompanied by a prescribed punishment, which could have you fasting regularly, getting whipped or paying penance. Masturbating would get you sentenced to 40 days' penitence – and the same punishment applied for anyone who tried, but failed, to have sex for fun. Lesbians got three years, while male gays got ten. Anyone who slept with their mother got the maximum – 15 years – and were only allowed to change their clothes on Sundays.

Medieval doctors often took a different approach, however. They saw sex as essential to health and warned that long-term celibacy could lead to a dangerous build-up of 'seminal humours'. They were heavily influenced by Galen, the first-century Classical doctor whose theories provided the backbone of European medical practice for centuries and whose cures, such as frequent bleeding, must have helped to kill millions. But Galen's influence on lovemaking medicine would have been popular: physicians recommended regular, though not excessive, sexual intercourse to release their patients' seminal humours. They added that the best moral way that single people and widows could stay healthy was to masturbate. Galen even recommended that physicians or midwives place hot poultices on the genitals of celibate women, causing them 'to experience orgasm, which would release the retained seed'. The Church naturally disagreed, saying masturbation could only be excused if it was unintentional. But how do you prove you were having a wet dream?

As for sex guides, the contemporary *De Secretis Mulierum* has a strong claim to be one of the most deceitful, nasty and wicked ever published. Its title translates as *The Secrets of Women* and the work purported to be about women's health. The contents, however, reflect the vicious paranoia of its misogynistic authors. It was written most probably in the thirteenth or early fourteenth century – possibly by Albertus Magnus, the theologian and scientist, or more likely by a disciple. It was published with the ostensible aim of helping to unravel the mysteries of creation for celibate monks and clerics who, theoretically at least, would be unfamiliar with a woman's reproductive parts. Subsequent editions carried additional comments by other scholars, and the book steadily grew into a bizarre testament to medieval Englishmen's warped attitudes to women and their bodies.

They seemed in particular to be rather frightened by the idea of sex with females, warning: 'The more women have sexual intercourse, the stronger they become, because they are made hot by the motion that the man makes during coitus. Further, male sperm is hot because it is of the same nature as air and when it is received by the woman it warms her entire body, so women are strengthened by this heat. On the other hand, men who have sex frequently are weakened by this act because they become exceedingly dried out.'

The authors also warned readers that they would be particularly unwise to go near women during their monthlies, because 'Women are so full of venom in their time of menstruation that they poison animals by their glance; they infect children in the cradle; they spot the cleanest mirror; and whenever men have sexual intercourse with them they are made leprous and sometimes cancerous.'

How Often?

Once a weak man

Dr Sylvester Graham, *Lectures to Young Men on Chastity* (c. 1837)

As a general rule it may be said to the healthy and robust, it were better for you not to exceed, in the frequency of your indulgences, the number of months in the year; and you cannot habitually exceed the number of weeks in the year without in some degree impairing your constitutional powers, shortening your lives and increasing your liability to disease and suffering – if indeed you do not thereby actually induce disease of the worst and most painful kind and at the same time transmit to your offspring an impaired constitution with strong and unhappy predispositions.

Four times a month, but never after a bath

Lyman B. Sperry, *Confidential Talks with Husband and Wife: a book of information and advice for the married and marriageable* (1900)

It may be safe to state that the ordinary man can safely indulge about four times a month. More than that would be excess for, perhaps, a large majority of civilized men and women. Sexual activity exhausts vitality; hence when one is fatigued, worried, digesting food or reacting from a bath, the vital energies are deeply engaged in important business. At such times, vitality says to sexual desire, 'I am otherwise engaged'.

Twice or thrice weekly. Or less

August Forel, *The Sexual Question: a scientific, psychological, hygiene and sociological study for the cultured classes* (1908)

The reformer Luther, who was a practical man, laid down the average of two or three connections a week in marriage, at the time of highest sexual power. I may say that my numerous observations as a physician have generally confirmed this rule, which seems to me to conform very well to the normal state to which man has become generally adapted during thousands of years.

Husbands who would consider this average as an imprescriptible right would, however, make wrong pretensions, for it is quite possible for a normal man to contain himself much longer, and it is his duty to do so, not only when his wife is ill, but also during menstruation and pregnancy.

Once a fortnight, or after sexy poems

Marie Stopes, *Married Love* (1918)

Women whose husbands, for instance, are abroad are the women from whom the best and most definitive evidence of a fundamental rhythm of feeling can be obtained. Such women, yearning daily for the tender comradeship and nearness of their husbands find, in addition, at particular times, an accession of longing for the close physical union of the final sex-act. Many such separated wives feel this; and those I have asked to keep note of the dates, have, with remarkable unanimity, told me that these times came specially just before and some week or so after the close of menstruation, coming, that is, about every fortnight ...

Many men, who can well practise restraint for 12 to 14 days, will find that one union will then thoroughly satisfy them; and if they have the good fortune to have healthy wives, they will find that the latter too have the desire for several unions in a day or two ... Expressed in general terms, my view may be formulated thus: the mutually best regulation of intercourse in marriage is to have three or four days of repeated unions, followed by about ten days without any unions at all, unless some external stimulus has stirred a mutual desire ...

In between these periods there may be additional special occasions when there springs up a mutual longing to unite. These will generally depend on some event in the lovers' lives which stirs their emotions; some memory of past passion, such as an anniversary of their wedding, or perhaps will be due to a novel, poem or picture which moves them deeply.

Beware, you'll have to keep it up

Theodoor Hendrik Van de Velde, *Ideal Marriage,*
Its Physiology and Technique (1928)

I would warn husbands not to recklessly habituate their wives to a degree of sexual frequency and intensity which they (the husbands) may be quite unable to keep up for any length of time. There are many women of moderate sexual temperament who keenly enjoy long festivals of erotic activity, in which husbands both give and demand their utmost, but who do not suffer or resent when the tempest abates and a calm follows.

But there are others, though they are perhaps less numerous among Northern races, who, when once introduced to the maximum of sexual pleasure cannot modify their desires when this maximum is no longer available. Then indeed the husband cannot exorcise the spirits he has invoked. He has the painful choice between chronic 'nerves' on his wife's part, which destroys marital peace and happiness, and equally chronic sexual overstrain and fatigue of his own.

Often no choice between these twin evils is possible and nerves, health, love and happiness are wrecked all round.

Five

BALI HIGH

Sexual matters, meanwhile, were rather more skilled and sensual in Southeast Asia.

Ancient Balinese culture revered sex as an important religious practice, which meant that Saturday-night quickies were ruled firmly out. Babies were made by mixing male and female fluids with the elements of air, fire, water, earth and space – along with the odd reincarnated soul. The magic only worked if the couple orgasmed at the same time. And they needed to perform synchronized sex consistently, as part of a regime of meditation, chanting and mutual pleasure. What's more, the quality of the sex was thought to affect the quality of the children. Hence the need for detailed manuals.

Bali's first erotic guides were written in around AD 900 at the latest, according to recent studies. They originated from Java, where Islam eventually suppressed them. But Islam never reached Bali, and the islanders revered their manuals as living texts, so generations of scholars and scribes updated them continually over many centuries. The books were called *Tutur* and could only be read as part of several years' study under close guidance from a teacher. *Tutur* were considered top-shelf stuff, and were usually marked with the words *aywa wera*: 'Do not disseminate indiscriminately.' The books also warned that if a man failed to follow their guidelines, then he was having sex not as a human but as an animal.

Foreplay was a lengthy business. One guide, *Rahasyasanggama*, stipulated that lovers must meditate themselves into a state of union with the divine before even starting sex – otherwise it would prove neither pleasurable nor productive. For first sexual encounters, the preliminaries could take weeks, if not months. Six stages were required: chatting up, to ensure compatibility; fantasizing (or in religious terms, visualizing the beloved day and night in order magically to attract the desired person); and then touching – a strict 30-day regime of caressing one part of their potential partner per day, running up one side of the body from big toe to forehead and then, when the moon turned from waxing to waning, coming back down the other side. Stage four required male suitors to pull their lovers towards them psychically through intense meditation: the length of time required was determined by the woman's tincture – it took three days if they were light-skinned, forty if they were dark. At this point, albino females must have been at something of a premium. Stage five, at last, was sex, though it demanded that the man be skilled and respectful in sexual relations, using (sadly unexplained) positions such as 'boxing', 'squirrel eats a nut', 'frog climbs a banana tree' and 'thrusting pig'. Stage six required the couple to start again, right from the beginning.

Even after that, properly married couples could not simply dive in willy-nilly whenever they pleased. The guides stressed that they had to practise sex at the right times. The rules forbade lovemaking on the wife's birthday, as well as the day before a full moon, and on new moons.

Across the water in Java, the ancient sex guides adopted early Islamic rules, which were based on the Prophet's guidance: no sex standing up, or sitting, or with the woman on top; no talk during intercourse; and sex during menstruation was banned because it created ugly children. Other written advice probably survived from older local folklore: you can tell the shape and size of a man's penis by looking at his thumb, while a woman's vagina reflects the shape of her mouth. Or perhaps they got those ones from the playground.

My Place or Yours?

How to pull

Philaenis, papyrus sex manual (2 BC)

Pick the woman's worst feature and then make it appear desirable. Tell an older woman that she looks young. Tell an ugly woman that she looks 'fascinating'.

Top womanizers

Kama Sutra of Vatsyayana (3rd century),
translated by Sir Richard F. Burton and F.F. Arbuthnot (1883)

The following generally obtain success with women:

Men well versed in the science of love
Raconteurs
Ones acquainted with women from their
     childhood
Guys who send women presents
Slick talkers
Men who have not loved other women previously
Chaps who know their weak points
Good-looking men
Men who have grown up with women
Men who live next door to women
Men who are devoted to sexual pleasures, even
     though these are with their own servants
The lovers of the nursemaid's daughters
Men who have been recently married
Men who like picnics and parties

Liberals
Men who are celebrated for being very strong
Enterprising and brave men
Men who are better looking, cleverer and kinder
than your husband

Girls go mad for burnt skulls

Ananga Ranga of Kalyanamalla (Stage of the Love God),
by the Indian poet Kalyan Mall (16th century)

Take a human skull from the cemetery or burning
ground on the eighth day of the moonlit fortnight
of the seventh month Ashvini (September–October),
expose it to fire, and collect the soot upon a plate
held over it; let this be drawn over the inner surface
of the eye-lids, instead of the usual antimony, and
the effect will be to fascinate all the women.

Turn yourself into a sex god

Kama Sutra of Vatsyayana (3rd century),
translated by Sir Richard F. Burton and F.F. Arbuthnot (1883)

First, get some fashionable gold hyena bones:
Good looks, good qualities, youth, and liberality are
the chief and most natural means of making a person
agreeable in the eyes of others. But in the absence of
these a man or a woman must have resort to artificial
means …

If the bone of a peacock or of a hyena be covered
with gold, and tied on the right hand, it makes a man
lovely in the eyes of other people.

Or smear either of these on your penis:

The application of a mixture of the leaf of the plant vatodbhranta, of the flowers thrown on a human corpse when carried out to be burnt, and the powder of the bones of the peacock.

The remains of a kite who has died a natural death, ground into powder, and mixed with honey.

Then enlarge yourself:

Rub your penis with the bristles of certain insects that live in trees, and then, after rubbing it for ten nights with oils, rub it with the bristles as before.

By continuing to do this a swelling will be gradually produced in the penis and you should then lie on a hammock with a hole in it, and hang it down through the hole. After this you should take away all the pain from the swelling by using cool concoctions. The swelling lasts for life.

How to be a failure

Perfumed Garden of Sheik Nefzaoui (16th century), translated by Sir Richard F. Burton

Know, O My Brother (to whom God be merciful), that a man who is misshapen, of coarse appearance, and whose member is short, thin and flabby, is contemptible in the eyes of women.

When such a man has a bout with a woman, he does not do her business with vigour and in a manner to give her enjoyment. He lays himself down upon her without previous toying, he does not kiss her, nor twine himself round her; he does not bite her, nor suck her lips, nor tickle her.

He gets upon her before she has begun longing for pleasure, and then he introduces with infinite trouble a member soft and nerveless. Scarcely has he commenced when he is already done for; he makes one or two movements, and then sinks upon the woman's breast to spend his sperm, and that is the most he can do. This done he withdraws his affair, and makes all haste to get down again from her.

Such a man is quick in ejaculation and slow as to erection; after the trembling, which follows the ejaculation of the seed, his chest is heavy and his sides ache.

Six

RENAISSANCE RENEGADES

The Renaissance in Europe revived not only the arts of painting and literature: from the late fifteenth century onwards, the sex-advice industry resurfaced and rapidly began to churn out international bestsellers, thanks to a vital new innovation – the printing press.

It had been invented in the mid-1450s and soon became available to entrepreneurs at relatively affordable prices. Ever since this point, the sex industry has relied on latest-tech tricks to pump its wares out faster than bureaucrats and lawmakers can ban them. The relationship has grown so close that the industry has even come to determine the direction that technology takes. In the 1970s, for example, no one knew which of the two rival home-videotape systems, Betamax or VHS, would dominate the market. For a while, it was neck and neck: Betamax had gone on sale first and many users believed it was better quality. But VHS was cheaper for film-making. Porn-movie producers predictably chose profits over art and went for VHS – which meant that masses of home-video buyers quickly followed suit, along with video-rental shops, which in the early days were exclusively pornographic. Bye-bye Betamax. Likewise, the internet would never have grown so rapidly without the financial success of its biggest market by far.

But this sort of innovation first occurred in Renaissance Italy, where many of the new-fangled printing presses were run by fly-by-night organizations. These were the pirate radio stations of their day, creating an anarchic free-for-all of new and seditious books. There were at least 1,300 publishers in sixteenth-century Italy and more than a third of them were based in Venice, which quickly became the main international marketplace, selling books to buyers from all over Europe. The Catholic Church's censors suddenly found they had trouble keeping up with the written word. Censorship scored a few spectacular successes but ultimately failed to restrict the free circulation of ideas. The average Venetian book's print run was probably around a thousand, though bestsellers may have run to 4,000 or more.

This wild, new info-frontier had few rules. If you could get away with it, then it was probably OK. Copyright hardly existed and libel laws were just as difficult to enforce. In 1540, preambles to legislation in Venice, where book publishing had become a huge source of local wealth, lamented that shoddy sleazebag printing was bringing disgrace to the city. Laws threatened to confiscate and burn cheap, pirated editions of popular works but these appear to have been merely the products of gesture-politics and no such crackdowns seem to have materialized (we can safely guess that plenty of bribes changed hands, though).

Amid the chaos, sex-manual writers thrived, producing barrow-loads of cheap, low-quality advice books that were poorly covered and bound – that's if the publishers bothered to bind them at all. Their size and type made them instantly recognizable as lascivious lit. The freely printed word also enabled eccentrics, quacks, visionaries and even churchmen to discuss their strange sex theories in intimate detail in private books, with little fear of criticism. Bizarre medical ideas were no rarity in the Renaissance, which evolved the theory of the wandering womb. If a woman became hysterical or misbehaved, this was blamed on her uterus having got dislodged and gone storming around, wreaking internal havoc. This, the theory claimed, was caused by the womb having been starved of sufficient intercourse or reproduction.

Other ideas included Giovanni Marinello's cure for premature ejaculation, in his 1563 *Medicine Pertinent to the Infirmities of Women*. This was based on the theory that women could not get pregnant if they did not orgasm, which presented a problem for premature-ejaculators. The answer for premature-ejaculators, therefore, was for them to tie string around their testicles. When the wife was ready to orgasm, she could untie the knot to receive hubby's semen – just so long as she was good at undoing knots at arm's length in the dark while orgasming and at the same time being careful not to injure her husband. Ouch.

But the most notorious of all the Renaissance love manuals did not rely on pseudo-science – it invented the simple formula of neat-drawing-plus-snappy-text that 450 years later was to make *The Joy of Sex* so successful. *I modi* (*The Ways*) was an explicitly illustrated guide to pleasurable sexual positions, which was first published in 1524. The first edition was simply a compilation of fine-art drawings of sixteen different sex acts by Giuliano Romano, the talented 25-year-old Mannerist protégé of Raphael. Pope Clement VII was enraged by it and ordered all copies burned. He also prohibited any form of distribution, imprisoned Romano and warned that anyone who published it again would be executed. In spite of this heavy deterrent, the book became an object lesson in the near impossibility of censoring pirate printers. A second edition emerged three years later, each picture now accompanied by a sonnet written by Pietro Aretino, a journalist, publicist, entrepreneur and art dealer who had become infamous as one of the lewdest wits in all Italy. The captions were forthright, to say the least. As for wit, perhaps tastes have changed. One reads: 'My legs are wrapped around your neck. Your cazzo's in my cul, it pushes and thrashes. I was in bed, but now I'm on this chest. What extreme pleasure you're giving me. But lift me on to the bed again – down here, my head hangs low, you'll do me in. The pain's worse than birth-pangs or shitting. Cruel love, what have you reduced me to?'

Ensuing years brought further bootleg copies, and eventually the number of positions grew to 31 as imitators added later and inferior drawings. After Aretino's death in 1556, the term 'Aretinian postures' became synonymous across Europe with acrobatic sex. The book was a popular read and won celebrity endorsement: Casanova recalls in his memoirs how he spent New Year's Eve 1753 performing Aretino's 'straight tree' position with a nun. He says it featured the man standing and holding the woman upside-down for mutual oral sex. It makes a change from singing 'Auld Lang's Syne'.

In Britain, in the wake of the Protestant Reformation, attitudes to marital sex had thawed in some denominations of the Church – especially among the Puritans. Their name has become a modern byword for all things strait-laced, but they actually believed pleasurable marital sex to be part of the holy sacrament. Early legal records in Puritan New England even record cases of husbands being admonished for failing to make love to their wives. Puritan marriage manuals completely contradicted Catholic distaste for spouse-on-spouse action. Writers such as William Whately, who published *A Bride Bush, or a Direction for Married Person* in 1616, and William Gouge (*Of Domestical Duties*, 1622) strongly promoted the right of married couples to enjoy 'mutual dalliances for pleasure's sake'. They also urged that 'husband and wife mutually delight each in the other,' maintain a 'fervent love' and exchange 'due benevolence one to another which is warranted and sanctified by God's word'.

Francis Rous, the provost of Eton College in Buckinghamshire, published a sermon in 1656 that sounds like the preamble to some medieval handbook of voyeurism. *The Mystical Marriage* was inspired by the prophet Isaiah's words, 'Fear not, for thy maker is thine husband'. Rous exhorted readers, 'Desire this husband ... Clear up thine eye and fix it on him as upon the fairest of men, the perfection of spiritual beautie ... accordingly fasten on him, not thine eye only, but thy mightiest love and hottest affection. Look on him so, that thou maist lust after him; for here it is a sin not to look as thou maist lust, and not to lust, having looked.'

It was powerful preaching, particularly from a Church that had not long before preached chastity as the only pure way. In the years approaching 1700, the general English market for sex advice was also getting stronger. We cannot know for certain what books were published or how many were bought, because the vast majority were printed as throwaway items, to be sold and read furtively. Samuel Pepys betrays himself in his diary as one of this growing band of secret sex-book stashers: 'Away to the Strand to my booksellers and bought that idle, roguish book, *L'Eschole des filles*, which I have bought in plain binding (avoiding the buying of it better bound) because I resolve, as soon as I have read it, to burn it, that it may not stand in the list of books, nor among them, to disgrace them if it should be found.'

But one book did more than survive: it became so popular that it was still in bookshops early in the twentieth century. It was called *Aristotle's Masterpiece*. The 4 BC Greek philosopher's *History of*

Animals, Parts of Animals, and Generation of Animals had provided the foundation both of Western zoology and Western sexology, and his influence was so great that almost anything attributed to him was believed. When the *Masterpiece* first came out, some enterprising publisher stuck Aristotle's name in the title, although only fragments of the information and misinformation it conveys can be traced to him. The first known edition is dated 1684 and was aimed at the common reader, the sort of literate lower-class person who bought ballads and almanacs. The text was primarily a collection of sexual folk wisdom, with hints on the positions to assume if you wanted to have a boy or a girl, and some rather bizarre pregnancy tests. The quality of the science is evident from this 'any other questions' exchange at the end of the book: 'Question: Why don't birds urinate? Answer: Because that superfluity which would be converted into urine, is turned into feathers.' Nevertheless, the *Masterpiece* went through at least 43 editions by 1800 and there were most likely many more, which ended up being hidden, burnt, torn up and otherwise lost by the likes of Pepys.

In France, Nicholas Venette (a pseudonym) became a contemporary rival to the *Masterpiece*. His *Tableau de l'amour conjugal* was published in France in 1696, not long after the *Masterpiece*. Its theme was similar but it felt more sophisticated and, initially, more salacious. It was translated in Britain in 1703 as *The Mysteries of Conjugal Love Reveald*, priced at six shillings, and soon became Europe's most popular sex guide – published in more than 100 editions and going well into the 20th century. Venette was a doctor and a father of 12. He was therefore doubly qualified to declare that the *Masterpiece*'s pregnancy tests – such as drinking honey and water at bedtime (a beating sense around the navel allegedly meant you'd conceived) – did not work.

Venette's opening literary gambit was one that became practically obligatory right up until the 1960s – getting your retaliation in first with a justification, excuse or apology about daring to write on such a touchy subject. He declared, 'If on the one hand, sin hath tacked shame to this knowledge; on the other, nature hath placed nothing there but what is delightful and pretty.' So please don't burn, jail, fine or sue me. Odd ideas? Try, 'From the right testicle cometh the male, and from the left, the female.' So if you tied the left one off, or lay on your right side while having sex, your chances of having a boy would increase. The book would have got him included on a *News of the World* hate-list for suggesting that women are sexually 'fit for commerce' when they reach their 13th birthday.

Venette had a few other strange notions, and in particular one that stemmed from a Galen-inspired belief, which was still popular in the 1700s, that masturbation was a decent way to get rid of excess sperm. Venette suggested that men are superior to woman because, by masturbating, they can renew their seed instead of allowing it to rot in their systems: 'She sometimes retains it lengthily in her testicles or in the horns of her uterus, where it becomes tainted and turns yellow, murky, or foul smelling, instead of white and clear as it was formerly. Unlike man, who, by polluting himself frequently, even during his sleep, benefits from a seed that is always renewed and never remains in his canals long enough to become corrupt.'

Women Who Make Good Lovers

It's all in the face

Yu Fang Mi Chueh
(Secret Codes of the Jade Room), c. AD 50

A woman with a small mouth and short fingers has a shallow porte feminine and she is easy to please. You can be sure that a woman must have big and thick labia if she has a big mouth and thick lips. If she has deep-set eyes, her porte feminine is bound to be deep too. If a woman has a pair of big, sparkling eyes, her porte feminine is narrow at its entrance, and yet roomy in the inner part. A woman with two dimples is tight and narrow down below.

Short (but normal) is best

Theodoor Hendrik Van de Velde, *Ideal Marriage,*
Its Physiology and Technique (1928)

Women of short stature and small bones can often meet all requirements in the flexibility and capacity of their vaginae. And their sexual vigour and efficiency are also conspicuous, not only in coitus but in their buoyant reaction to the mental and physical stress and strain of menstruation, pregnancy and parturition, their fine flow of milk and easy and frequent conception (note the saying among the English common people: 'Little women – big breeders').

In short, little women approximate most often to the typical womanly ideal. But of course this is only

the case when this small stature is perfectly propor-
tionate throughout and when the sexual development is adequate. When the small stature is due to
some form of abnormality it is more than likely that
the genitals will show serious defects structurally
and functionally, in some way or other.

Sweaty's sexy

Fang Nei Chi (Records of the Bedchamber),
Sui Dynasty (AD 590–618)

Suitable women are naturally tender and docile and
of gentle mien. Their hairs are of a silky black, their
skin is soft and their bones fine. They are neither too
tall nor too short, neither too fat nor too thin. The
lips of the vulva should be thick and large. Their
groins should not be covered with hair and the vagina
should be moist. Their age should be between 25 and
30 and they should not yet have borne a child.

During coition their vaginas should emit abundant
liquid. Their bodies should move so that they cannot restrain themselves. Drenched in sweat, they
succumb to the motions of their man. Women
endowed with these qualities will never harm a man,
even if he himself is ignorant of the correct way of
sexual intercourse.

Small-breasted, shrill hairy heaven

Nicholas Venette, *The Mysteries of
Conjugal Love Reveald* (1703)

Woman, hot in constitution and vehemently desirous
of commerce with man, is easily distinguished by
those versed in the nature of sex. In order to inform
the ignorant, the breasts of such a woman are generally very small, but at the same time conveniently
plump and hard. There is a profusion of hair about
her privities occasioned by the extraordinary heat in
those parts. The hair of the head is short and inclin-
able to curl, her voice is shrill and loud; she is cold of
speech, cruel and oppressive to those of her own sex
and unsteady in her devotion.

She is very complaisant and obliging in her behaviour towards men, but especially to those of her
friends and acquaintance; she is of florid complexion,
upright in the gesture of her body and more inclined
to be lean than fat. She is sometimes given to excess
in wine.

We may be sure, a woman answering this description, is extremely lecherous; and one who, in the act
of coition, fulfils her desire greatly to the content
and pleasure of the many having carnal knowledge of
her ... Let me add that the libidinous woman smells
not so rank when she perspires as other women do.

Hefty and breastless: mmm

Fang Nei Chi (Records of the Bedchamber),
Sui Dynasty (AD 590–618)

A man should select for his sexual partners young women whose breasts have not yet developed and who are well covered with flesh. They should have hair as fine as silk and small eyes in which the pupil and the white are clearly separated. Face and body should be smooth and speech harmonious. All her joints should be well covered and her bones should not be large. She should either have no pubic and axillary hair at all or such hair should be fine and smooth.

Is she a virgin? Four tests

Albertus Magnus, *De Secretis Mulierum*
(*The Secrets of Women*) (c. 1478)

If you want to determine if a virgin has been corrupted, grind up the flowers of a lily and the yellow particles that are between the flowers, and give her this substance to eat. If she is corrupt, she will urinate immediately.

Another way to tell is to have her urinate on a certain kind of grass which is commonly known as 'papel de mane'. If it becomes dry she is corrupt. You can also take the fruit of a lettuce and place it in front of her nose, and she will urinate immediately.

The signs of chastity are as follows: shame, modesty, fear, a faultless gait and speech, casting eyes down before men and the acts of men. Some women are so clever, however, that they know how to resist detection by these signs, and in this case a man should turn to their urine. The urine of virgins is clear and lucid, sometimes white, sometimes sparkling. Corrupted women have a muddy urine because of the rupture of the aforementioned skin, and male sperm appear at the bottom of this urine.

There are still other ways to tell if a virgin has been corrupted. If a girl's breasts point downwards, this is a sign that she has been corrupted, because at the moment of impregnation the menses move upwards to the breasts and the added weight causes them to sag. If a man has sexual intercourse with a woman and experiences no sore on his penis and no difficulty of entry, this is a sign that she was first corrupted. However, a true sign of the woman's virginity is if it is difficult to perform the act and it causes a sore on his member.

If it's too late, how to restore virginity

The Book of Women's Love,
a medieval Hebrew women's health guide

Take myrtle leaves and boil them well with water until only a third part remains; then, take nettles without prickles and boil them in this water until a third remains. She must wash her secret parts with this water in the morning and at bedtime, up to nine days.

And if it's an emergency

Take nutmeg and grind to a powder; put it in that place and virginity will be restored immediately.

Seven

MASTURBATION MANIA

From the early 1700s onwards, the innocent practice of self-love became synonymous with crippling illnesses, moral decay and hideous death. Why?

We can thank an anonymous quack from about 1710 for first pointing the finger of suspicion at the hairy palm of lone vice. Whoever the author was, snappy titles were not their strong point. Their pamphlet was called *Onania, or the heinous sin of self-pollution, And in all its frightful consequences, in both sexes, considered with physical and spiritual advice to those who have already injur'd themselves by this abominable practice. And seasonable admonition to the youth of the nation [of both sexes] and whose tuition they are under, whether parents, guardians, masters or mistresses.* In it, the author simply invented a new cause of widespread diseases by making a spurious connection between masturbation and the biblical story of Onan.

In *Solitary Sex: a cultural history of masturbation*, the historian Thomas Laqueur alleges that *Onania*'s author was an amateur doctor and surgeon called Dr

Marten (not he of footwear fame). Once Marten had invented the scourge of Onanism-related illnesses, claims Laqueur, he started to offer a range of steeply priced cures, such as 'strengthening tincture' and 'prolific powder'. If that is true, it makes Marten an early pioneer of the widespread modern pharmaceutical company marketing trick of creating a new disease, scaring people about it in the press, and then launching (fortuitously) a costly cure. Newly minted health problems such as Social Anxiety Disorder and Information Fatigue Syndrome may thus be merely latter-day versions of masturbation.

The biblical Onan gets a bad press from here onwards. It's not justified: in the Old Testament story, he was instructed by God to impregnate the widow of his recently dead brother – an ancient Hebrew tradition that aimed to ensure there were family heirs. Onan wasn't keen on perpetuating his brother's bloodline, so he pulled out of his sister-in-law at the last minute. God struck him dead 'for spilling his seed on the ground' but he had committed coitus interruptus, not masturbation. Society was not prepared to let the facts ruin a good scare story, though, and masturbation mania swiftly began to take off. Marten's pamphlet became wildly popular, disseminating the belief across Europe that Onanism was the cause of diseases ranging from tuberculosis to third-stage syphilis. By 1750, it had been published in 19 editions and sold 38,000 copies.

Soon came the copycats. In 1717, a hugely popular free handout, *Practical Schemes for the Secret*

Disease and Broken Constitutions, was published with a new section on self-abuse by the most popular contemporary advisor on painkillers in Great Britain, the self-styled Mr Anodyne Necklace. He subsequently published similar rants: *The Crime of Onan*, *Eromania* and a further follow-up, *Eromania; on the crimes of those two unhappy brothers Er and Onan*. Other publishers' titles included *Onania displayd*, in which the word Onanism was originally coined.

In 1758, Samuel Tissot, a Swiss doctor, threw more fuel on the fire by publishing, *L'Onanisme, ou dissertation physique sur les maladies produites par la masturbation*, which, through its hundreds of editions, variations and imitators spread further fear of the evils of self-pleasure and 'postmasturbatory disease' throughout the Continent. He argued from the perspective of 'medical science' that the unnatural loss of semen weakened mind and body and led to insanity. The book was still in print as recently as 1905. Along with Marten's work, Tissot's writings moved like some terrible contagion across the Atlantic to America. Their influence there, as we shall see, was of another magnitude entirely.

Loose Women

Blondes

Giovanni Sinibaldi, *Rare Verities,
the Cabinet of Venus Unlock'd* (1658)

All women are lascivious, but auburn blondes the most … A little straight forehead denotes an unbridled appetite in lust.

Actors' wives

Kama Sutra of Vatsyayana (3rd century),
translated by Sir Richard F. Burton and F.F. Arbuthnot (1883)

The following are the women who are easily gained over:

Women who stand at the doors of their houses
Women who are always looking out on the street
Women who sit chatting in their neighbour's house
A woman who is always staring at you
A woman who looks sideways at you
A woman whose husband has taken another wife without any just cause
A woman who hates her husband, or who is hated by him
A woman who has nobody to look after her, or keep her in check
A woman who has not had any children
A woman whose family or caste is not well known

A woman whose children are dead

A woman who is very fond of society

A woman who is apparently very affectionate
with her husband

The wife of an actor

A widow

A poor woman

A woman who likes fun

The wife of a man with many younger brothers

A vain woman

A woman whose husband is inferior to her in
rank or abilities

One who is proud of her skill in the arts

A woman mentally disturbed by her husband's
stupidity

A woman who has been married in her infancy
to a rich man, and not liking him when she
grows up, desires a man possessing a
disposition, talents, and wisdom suitable to
her own tastes

A woman who is slighted by her husband
without any cause

A woman who is not respected by other
women of the same rank or beauty as
herself

A woman whose husband is devoted to
travelling

The wife of a jeweller

A jealous woman

A covetous woman

An immoral woman

A barren woman
A lazy woman
A cowardly woman
A humpbacked woman
A dwarfish woman
A deformed woman
A vulgar woman
An ill-smelling woman
A sick woman
An old woman

Women only want one thing

Perfumed Garden of Sheik Nefzaoui (16th century),
translated into English by Sir Richard F. Burton

The woman loves the man only for the sake of coition. His member should, therefore, be of ample dimensions and length. Such a man ought to be broad in the chest, and heavy in the crupper; he should know how to regulate his emission, and be ready as to erection; his member should reach to the end of the canal of the female, and completely fill the same in all its parts. Such a one will be well beloved by women.

On the other hand

Dr William Acton, *Functions and Disorders of the Reproductive Organs* (1858)

The majority of women (happily for them) are not very much troubled with sexual feelings of any kind. What men are habitually, women are only exceptionally.

And if you're not convinced ...

George Napheys, *The Transmission of Life: counsels on the nature and hygiene of the masculine function* (1871)

Only in rare circumstances do women feel one tenth of the sexual feeling which is familiar to most men. Many of them are entirely frigid and not even in marriage do they ever perceive any real desire.

Eight

CARLILE, THE CONTRACEPTIVE CONVICT

At the beginning of the nineteenth century, conventional Christian belief still held that Onan's true crime, practising coitus interruptus, was not the only method of contraception that might make God strike you dead – they all could.

Anything that prevented conception was banned in the belief that sex was for procreation. Fornication put you in the fast lane to the eternal flames. So who better to write the first published book on contraception than a convicted blasphemer? Even better, he composed it while in jail.

Richard Carlile, the author, was never really interested in sex books, but years later he told a rather pat anecdote about his moment of revelation. One day in 1812, when he was a young tinsmith, he was browsing at a Plymouth market bookstall and watched a serving maid arrive to pick up a book for her mistress. Carlile saw it was the *Masterpiece*, and that the maid had 'looked up quite cunning, as if she had got a certain prize ... and scampered away delighted'. Carlile said he knew the *Masterpiece* was tosh – and that it didn't even mention contraception.

So he resolved to produce a genuinely useful sex manual that could properly educate the poor young maids of this world.

It's just the sort of idea that might have struck hundreds of people, but who really ever has the time or inclination? Thirteen years later, as a bookseller, radical publisher and journalist, Carlile found himself with both. He was serving six years in Dorchester prison for blasphemy (three years for the offence, three for being unable to pay the fine), having been prosecuted by the Evangelical Vice Society for selling Tom Paine's *The Age of Reason*. But he was still working and publishing, so he wrote an article, 'What is Love?', for his sixpenny journal, *The Republican*. A year later, in 1826, he published an extended version as a pamphlet, called *Every Woman's Book*, with a frontispiece featuring a full-frontal nude and unashamed Adam and Eve.

Carlile was actually a self-confessed prude, but his greatest passion was hatred of Christianity, so the book was his chance to attack the Church. It did not go into the details of techniques and tickles, but gave ordinary women clear advice on using contraceptive sponges, as well as promoting the pleasures of sex (though Onanism was, once again, a complete no-no). Birth control was, Carlile believed, a political tool – it could help to save poor families from growing too large and prevent young women falling pregnant and facing the devil's dilemma of single motherhood or forced marriage. The book had social revolutionary aspects, too, championing free heterosexual intercourse, sexual rights for women and male–female relationships outside marriage. Sexual intercourse should be accepted for what it is, he said, not simply as a means of reproduction but as a self-fulfilling pleasure in itself. It should, he argued, 'be made a pleasure independent of the dread of a conception'.

The book got Carlile burned in effigy, threatened with drenching and denounced in a newspaper as the 'pedagogue pander of lust'. It was popular, too, selling 10,000 copies in three years, with six editions published in Carlile's lifetime and at least three afterwards. It was still selling strongly in the 1830s. Why did he get away with publishing it? Perhaps the authorities did not want a repeat of his trial for selling Paine's *The Age of Reason*. As soon as he had been convicted and jailed, his wife committed the same crime and was jailed. Then his sister did the same. Then a steady flow of objectors followed suit, until the law effectively became unworkable and the authorities left Paine's book alone. Carlile's success allowed a spot of liberal rot to set in: *Every Woman's Book* inspired several other authors. In 1832, two contraceptive tracts, Robert Dale Owen's *Moral Physiology* and Charles Knowlton's *Fruits of Philosophy, or the private companion of young married people*, were published. Knowlton published his anonymously and in it recommended post-coital douching. Owen, who became an American Congressman and co-founded the Smithsonian Institution, recommended coitus inter-ruptus. Between them, the books dominated birth-control ideas in Britain for the next 40 years.

Don't Fancy Yours Much: Rough Sex Partners

Beware dishevelled hair

Fang Nei Chi (Records of the Bedchamber),
Sui Dynasty (AD 590–618)

Dishevelled hair and coarse face, elongated neck and a protruding Adam's apple, irregular teeth and manly voice, a large mouth and long nose, eyes which are bloodshot or yellowish, long hairs on upper lip or cheeks resembling whiskers, large and protruding bones, yellowish hair and little flesh and long and stiff pubic hairs. Such women are harmful to the man. Sexual intercourse with these will rob a man of his health and vigour.

Thin hair's bad, too

Nicholas Venette, *The Mysteries of
Conjugal Love Reveald* (1703)

A woman of cold constitution has great and flabby breasts, is very thin of hair about the privy parts, which are placed so low and near the anus that man always finds a difficulty in entering her body. She is childish in disposition, timorous in speech, easy in belief and happy in a gentle temper. She is pious and pitiful of another's misery.

Take it for granted that a woman of this condition is never provoked to copulation by lascivious wishes and desires. She rather suffers the embraces of a man than likes them and, having little enjoyment herself, gives little pleasure to the person lying with her. Her perspiration is rank. She is more inclined to be fat than lean, is pale and easy to be impregnant.

And as for woolly hair ...

Perfumed Garden of Sheik Nefzaoui (16th century), translated into English by Sir Richard F. Burton

The woman who merits the contempt of the men is ugly and garrulous; her hair is woolly, her forehead projecting, her eyes are small and blear, her nose enormous, the lips lead-colored, the mouth large, the cheeks wrinkled and she shows gaps in her teeth.

Her cheekbones shine purple, and she sports bristles on her chin, her head sits on a meager neck, with overdeveloped tendons; her shoulders are contracted and her chest is narrow, with flabby pendulous breasts, and her belly is like an empty leather-bottle, with the navel standing out like a heap of stones; her flanks are shaped like arcades; the bones of her spinal column may be counted; there is no flesh upon her croup; her vulva is large and cold, and exhales an odor of carrion; it is hairless, pale and wet, with a long hard, greasy clitoris projecting out of it. Finally, such a woman has large knees and feet, big hands and emaciated legs. A woman with such blemishes can give no pleasure to men in general, and least of all to him who is her husband or who enjoys her favors.

The man who approaches a woman like that with his member in erection will find it presently soft and relaxed, as though he was only close to a beast of burden. May God keep us from a woman of that description.

Banned women: leave that aunt alone

Old Testament, Leviticus, chapter 18

Mother
Father's wife
Maternal and/or paternal sister, from the
    household or outside
Son's or daughter's daughter
Paternal aunt
Maternal aunt
Uncle's wife
Daughter-in-law
Brother's wife
Bad twosomes: woman and her daughter;
    woman and her sister

If they smell, steer clear

Kama Sutra of Vatsyayana (3rd century),
translated by Sir Richard F. Burton and F.F. Arbuthnot (1883)

Lepers
Lunatics
Women who can't keep secrets
Those who publicly express desire for sex
Women who are extremely white
Women who are extremely black
Bad-smelling women
Near relations
Female friends
Women who lead the life of an ascetic
Wives of relations, friends, of learned
   Brahmans, and of the king

Never marry these women

Koka Shastra (*The Scripture of Koka*),
by the Indian poet Kokkoka (12th century)

Red-heads

Any girl named after a mountain, a tree, a river
or a bird

Ones with rough hands or feet

Ones who sigh, laugh or cry at meals

Any girl with inverted nipples, beards, uneven
breasts, flap ears, spindle legs or who is
scrawny

Girls whose big toes are disproportionately
small

Girls who make the ground shake when they
walk past

And women a wife should shun

Whores, witches, begging nuns, women who
hang round with actors, and sellers of herbs
or potions

Nine

DRYSDALE'S REVOLUTIONARY DREAM

If you wished to play the rebel in mid-Victorian Britain, one safe strategy was to publish a radical sex guide.

George Drysdale published his while he was a medical student at Edinburgh University in 1854. He rather spoilt the anarchic effect by publishing it anonymously because, it transpired, he did not want to upset his mum. He also failed to rake in any profits from his sex manual. Carlile's book had set him up for life, but Drysdale's actually cost him money. He had a private income and decided that he could afford to sell it relatively cheaply – at two shillings and six – to the sort of readership he wanted to reach.

The book, *Elements of Social Science: physical, sexual and natural religion*, thudded in at 400 closely printed, densely written pages. This was no bedside book. Its ideas were similar to Carlile's, but much more extreme. In spite of its heavy physical and intellectual weight, the book sold more than 90,000 copies within 50 years. Perhaps it made a cost-effective doorstop. Drysdale called on men and women alike to meet their natural duty to 'exercise duly their sexual organs'. In his 'law of exercise', Drysdale argued that sex was a sacred panacea, while abstinence could cause untold physical and mental damage. He added that, 'Ignorance of the necessity for sexual intercourse to the health and virtue of both man and woman is the most fundamental error in medical and moral philosophy'. He was the first doctor in England to write in defence of contraception, at a time when *The Lancet* condemned it as a practice that reduced sex to a transaction where women acted as prostitutes and men were mere masturbators.

He also called for a world of free love, questioning why people should be bound together for life just because they'd got the hots for each other. If it sounds like the pot-addled sermon of a Sixties swinger, then bear in mind that Drysdale also entertained some rather dodgy and mixed-up theories. Prostitution should be banned and married couples should be careful not to overindulge in sex, he argued. And while on the one hand, he said that juveniles should practise sexual intercourse, on the other, self-sex was completely out.

It's a sad irony that Drysdale's entire approach was so heavily biased against Onanism. Fear of it had driven him to the brink of a suicidal breakdown as a young man, and his book served ultimately to refine this paranoia and then sell it on to others at a bargain price. The young Drysdale had become convinced that his health was imperilled by spermatorrhoea – excessive and debilitating loss of sperm through wet dreams and masturbation. The historian

Michael Bush suggests that Drysdale used his own life story in his book, in the case study of a young man who, unable to curtail his masturbatory impulses, falls into despair. In search of a cure, he takes long walking holidays across Europe. In desperation, he has his genitals cauterized. Eventually he finds salvation in the simple prescription of regular sexual intercourse. Drysdale's book may well have been more an evangelistic autobiography than a revolutionary tract.

How to Do Foreplay

Not until you're married

Newnes, *Manual of Marriage* (1964)

It can be said with confidence that any pre-marital manipulation of the genital organs is overstepping the mark, and these might well be thought to include the breasts.

Haste makes waste

Harland Long, MD,
Sane Sex Life and Sane Sex Living (1919)

Regarding the first part of the act, let it be said that here, above all the situations in the world, 'haste makes waste'. Put that down as the most fundamental fact in the whole affair! Right here is where ninety-nine one-hundredths of all the troubles of married life begin!

Treat her like basil

Perfumed Garden of Sheik Nefzaoui (16th century),
translated into English by Sir Richard F. Burton

Woman is like a fruit, which will not yield its sweetness until you rub it between your hands. Look at the basil plant; if you do not rub it warm with your fingers it will not emit any scent. Do you not know that the amber, unless it be handled and warmed, keeps hidden within its pores the aroma contained in it?

It is the same with woman. If you do not animate her with your toying, intermixed with kissing, nibbling and touching, you will not obtain from her what you are wishing; you will feel no enjoyment when you share her couch, and you will waken in her heart neither inclination nor affection, nor love for you; all her qualities will remain hidden.

Thirteen steps from wrists to riding

Mawangdui medical manuscripts (200–300 BC)

Clasp her hands and move your palms up the
 outside of her wrists
Stroke the elbows
Move up the underarms
Then work on the chest, between neck and
 breasts
Go to the abdomen
Stroke the pelvic region
Mount her at the waist
Observe her genitalia
Stroke her navel
Move your hands downwards
Skim her pubic mound
Penetrate her
And ride ...

Woo - and win

Marie Stopes, *Married Love* (1918)

A man does not woo and win woman once and for all when he marries her: he must woo her before every separate act of coitus.

Sing together (gesticulations optional)

Kama Sutra of Vatsyayana (3rd century),
translated by Sir Richard F. Burton and F.F. Arbuthnot (1883)

In the pleasure-room, decorated with flowers, and fragrant with perfumes, attended by his friends and servants, the citizen should receive the woman, who will come bathed and dressed, and will invite her to take refreshment and to drink freely.

He should then seat her on his left side, and holding her hair, and touching also the end and knot of her garment, he should gently embrace her with his right arm. They should then carry on an amusing conversation on various subjects, and may also talk suggestively of things which would be considered as coarse, or not to be mentioned generally in society.

They may then sing, either with or without gesticulations, and play on musical instruments, talk about the arts, and persuade each other to drink. At last when the woman is overcome with love and desire, the citizen should dismiss the people that may be with him, giving them flowers, ointments, and betel leaves, and then when the two are left alone, they should proceed.

Wear slippers

Giovanni Sinibaldi, *Rare Verities,
the Cabinet of Venus Unlock'd* (1658)

Cold feet are a powerful hindrance to coition –
couples should wear soft, noiseless slippers.

Thirty days of foreplay – or seventy if she's dark

Sad Smara (*Six Stages of Love*) (Bali, 19th century)

Stage one: use love talk on the woman you desire. Be
careful to use beautiful language to evoke her desire.

Stage two: watch her closely and memorize her
features. Use these for attraction magic in which you
mentally call her to accompany you in all activities. If
you are totally focused, the woman will come to you
directly.

Stage three: this is a strict regime of touching her
body, according to the stage of the moon, in order to
arouse her. From the first to the fifteenth days of
the waxing moon, start at her feet and move up the
right side of her body to her head, touching in turn
the big toe, sole, heel, ankle, calf, knee, thigh, hip,
genitals, navel, breast, chin, lips, eyes and forehead.
Once the moon begins to wane, reverse this list,
moving down her left side. If you always touch the
correct body part, accompanied by flattery and
sweet talk, she will be aroused with an insatiable
desire for you.

Stage four: your yogic meditation should attract your beloved emotionally and physically, through thought-transfer. The number of days you must meditate depends on the colour of her skin. If she is pale, it takes three days. Medium-toned women take seven days and nights. Dark take forty nights and days. Avoid sexual contact with other women. If the yoga is successful, you will be able to visualize yourself having sex with her on a particular day, at which point she will either come to you or, if she can't, weep unrelentingly.

Stage five: this requires you to be skilled and respectful in sexual relations, satisfying the woman as if she is hungry and must be given food, but with neither too much nor too little. The acts used to sexually arouse a woman are called boxing, squirrel eats a nut, frog climbs a banana tree and thrusting pig (*sadly, these are not described, but you can guess*).

Stage six: do it all over again.

Five steps to heaven: the tao of dalliance

Mawangdui medical manuscripts (200–300 BC)

The essential task in the pleasures of play is to be slow and prolonged. If only he can be slow and prolonged the woman then is greatly pleased. She treats him with the closeness she feels for her brothers, and loves him like her father and mother. One who has mastered this tao deserves to be called a heavenly gentleman …

First, when her chi rises and her face becomes flushed, slowly exhale

Second, when her nipples become hard and her nose perspires slowly embrace her

Third, when her tongue slowly spreads and becomes lubricious, slowly press her

Fourth, when secretions appear below and her thighs are damp, slowly take hold of her

Fifth, when her throat is dry and she swallows saliva, slowly agitate her

Keep working at it

Dr Walter Robie, *Sex and Life* (1916)

No woman is so glacial that she will not respond to the tactful insistence of the right man ... The husband should not rest easy, nor should the wife allow him to, until they have discovered the methods and positions which give her the greatest pleasure and completest orgasm.

Ten

MANUAL MARTYRS

Despite Carlile and Drysdale's best efforts, the moral tide continued to pull towards a new era of superficial primness: Victorianism.

The plain-speaking sexuality of Venette's *Mysteries of Conjugal Love Reveald* and the *Masterpiece* steadily became watered down through the second half of the 1800s to the point where new editions no longer discussed sex openly or explained the anatomy of the genitals. Instead, words of warning were added.

The moral clampdown began to claim victims. Charles Knowlton's *The Fruits of Philosophy* had for 40 years been openly sold as a mainstay of contraceptive advice on both sides of the Atlantic when, in the 1870s, a Bristol printer was sentenced to two years' prison with hard labour for selling it. In response, a pair of freethinkers, Charles Bradlaugh and Annie Besant, decided to resist, by setting up the Free Thought Publishing Company to provoke a test case. In 1877 they republished the book in a new, cheap edition, and told the police what they were doing. To provide some sort of moral context, the age of consent in Britain at the time was 13 and was only raised to 16 in 1885 – and then after fierce resistance. Incest was only made illegal in Britain in 1908.

The case of *Regina v Charles Bradlaugh and Annie Besant* proved a lengthy business. They were charged with publishing material that was 'likely to deprave or corrupt those whose minds are open to immoral influences' and were initially sentenced to six months' imprisonment. The pair won their appeal against conviction in the High Court, but the greater victory was the PR coup that the pair had managed to pull off: their case threw birth control 'on to the breakfast tables of the English middle classes', said one observer.

Sales of *The Fruits of Philosophy* shot up from fewer than 1,000 a year to more than 100,000 in the three months preceding the trial and they remained high afterwards. Besant became a contraceptive celebrity and wrote her own book, *The Law of Population*. Besant had personal reasons to publicize birth control – she had been brought up poor and married young, at 19, to an Anglican clergyman. By 23, she was the mother of two and feeling trapped. She'd had enough of her husband's preaching and refused to go to communion, so he threw her out of the marital home. Then she joined the anti-Church National Secular Society, met Bradlaugh and they began an affair. Early editions of her book followed Carlile's example and recommended the sponge; later ones promoted two new methods – the Dutch cap and soluble pessaries. The manufacture of spermicides, condoms and caps grew rapidly.

But even after the Bradlaugh trial, prosecutions continued against contraceptive guides. In 1878, Edward Truelove, a 67-year-old rationalist publisher, got four months' jail for publishing Robert Dale Owen's *Moral Physiology*. And in 1892, a Newcastle phrenologist received a sentence of one month's hard labour for selling H.H. Allbutt's 1886 *The Wife's Handbook: how a woman should order herself during pregnancy with hints on other matters of importance, necessary to be known by married women.* The work, a big hit in America, contained a four-page review of contraceptive methods, including: 'coughing (unreliable), coitus interruptus (hurtful to the nervous system in many persons) and condoms (a very certain check)'. Dr Allbutt had been struck off from the British medical register in 1887 – for selling the book at 'such a low price', rather than for writing abject nonsense.

Both Bradlaugh and Besant later moved into politics – Bradlaugh was elected Britain's first freethinker MP in 1880 but steadfastly refused to take the Commons' Christian oath and so was repeatedly expelled. Besant helped the match-girls at Bryant & May to organize a union to fight against their dreadful working conditions. Subsequently she became a religious mystic, joining Madame Blavatsky's Eastern-occult based Theosophist movement and moving to India in 1880. There, she met 13-year-old Jiddu Krishnamurti, whom she decided was the reincarnation of Buddha, and took him on a two-year tour of England and America to proclaim him to the world as a new messiah. Krishnamurti later said it was a case of mistaken identity. Besant also collaborated with Indian independence agitators, became president of the Indian Home Rule League and was interned by the British during the First World War. She died in India in 1933, but her name lives on – one of Bombay's main thoroughfares is called after her.

Honeymoon Bliss

It's an investment

Eustace Chesser, *Love Without Fear* (1942)

The groom who is considerate and patient on his wedding night will be repaid a thousand times in years to come.

Control your propensities

John Harvey Kellogg,
Plain Facts for Old and Young (1877)

Bear this fact in mind, young man. Curb your passions. Control your propensities, and years hence you will look back upon your conduct with a satisfaction which will increase your self-respect. The brutal conduct of husbands, even on the first night of marriage, not infrequently entails upon their wives a lifetime of suffering. Such individuals are quite unworthy the name of men. They are fit only to be classed with the rakes who violate defenseless virgins, and treat women as though they were made for no other purpose than the gratification of the beastly propensities of brutal men.

Steer clear of spice and sleep on the floor

Kama Sutra of Vatsyayana (3rd century),
translated by Sir Richard Burton and F.F. Arbuthnot (1883)

For the first three days after marriage, the girl and her husband should sleep on the floor, abstain from sexual pleasures, and eat their food without seasoning.

Some say that the husband should play it cool and not speak to her for three days, but others believe that the girl may be discouraged by seeing him spirit-less like a pillar, and, becoming dejected, she may begin to despise him as a eunuch.

For the next seven days they should bathe amidst the sounds of auspicious musical instruments, should decorate themselves, dine together, and welcome their relatives as well as to those who may have come to witness their marriage.

On the night of the tenth day the man should begin in a secluded place with soft, winning words, and thus create confidence in the girl. But he should abstain at first from sexual pleasures.

Women, being of a tender nature, want tender beginnings, and when they are forcibly approached by men with whom they are but slightly acquainted, they sometimes suddenly become haters of sexual connection, and sometimes even haters of the male sex.

Do give her your hand ...

Helena Wright, *The Sex Factor in Marriage* (1930)

In the first days of marriage ... an orgasm induced by the husband's hand, and entirely by way of clitoris sensation, may be a kind and gentle way of introducing a timid and perhaps frightened girl to a happy sex life.

Horrid shock for the bride

Ida Craddock, *The Wedding Night* (1900)

There is a wrong way and there is a right way to pass the wedding night. In the majority of cases, no genital union at all should be attempted, or even suggested, upon that night. To the average young girl, virtuously brought up, the experience of sharing her bedroom with a man is sufficient of a shock to her previous maidenly habits, without adding to her nervousness by insisting upon the close intimacies of genital contact.

And, incredible as it may sound to the average man, she is usually altogether without the sexual experience which every boy acquires in his dream-life. The average, typical girl does not have erotic dreams. In many cases, too, through the prudishness of parents – a prudishness which is positively criminal – she is not even told beforehand that genital union will be required of her.

If you will first thoroughly satisfy the primal passion of the woman, which is affectional and maternal (for the typical woman mothers the man she loves), and if you will kiss and caress her in a gentle, delicate and reverent way, especially at the throat and bosom, you will find that, little by little (perhaps not the first night nor the second night, but eventually, as she grows accustomed to the strangeness of the intimacy), you will, by reflex action from the bosom to the genitals, successfully arouse within her a vague desire for the entwining of the lower limbs, with ever closer and closer contact, until you melt into one another's embrace at the genitals in a perfectly natural and wholesome fashion.

As to the clitoris, this should be simply saluted, at most, in passing, and afterwards ignored as far as possible; for the reason that it is a rudimentary male organ, and an orgasm aroused there evokes a rudimentary male magnetism in the woman, which appears to pervert the act of intercourse, with the result of sensualizing and coarsening the woman.

Within the duller tract of the vagina, after a half-hour, or, still better, an hour of tender, gentle, self-restrained coition, the feminine, womanly, maternal sensibilities of the bride will be aroused, and the magnetism exchanged then will be healthful and satisfying to both parties. A woman's orgasm is as important for her health as a man's is for his. And the bridegroom who hastens through the act without giving the bride the necessary half-hour or hour to come to her own climax, is not only acting selfishly; he is also sowing the seeds of future ill-health and permanent invalidism in his wife.

As to the bride, I would say: bear in mind that it is part of your wifely duty to perform pelvic movements during the embrace, riding your husband's organ gently, and, at times, passionately, with various movements, up and down, sideways, and with a semi-rotary movement, resembling the movement of the thread of a screw upon a screw. These movements will add greatly to your own passion and your own pleasure, but they should not be dwelt in thought for this purpose. They should be performed for the express purpose of conferring pleasure upon your husband, and you should carefully study the results of various movements, gently and tenderly performed, upon him.

How considerate

Dr Alex Comfort, *The Joy of Sex* (1972)

Most girls are now carefully stretched beforehand by their considerate boyfriends.

Eleven

KAMA SUTRA CHAMELEON

From India, thanks to an English adventurer straight out of *Ripping Yarns*, comes a book that has become a legend of complex Oriental couplings and non-stop priapic action.

The *Kama Sutra* is Britain's best-known love manual, though relatively few people actually saw the book during its 80-year English publication ban or have bothered to read it since.

Sir Richard Burton, the Victorian explorer, linguist, ethnologist, diplomat and soldier (rather than the Welsh actor), is one of history's most eminent and dedicated manual men. Among his great adventures, he co-discovered Lake Tanganyika, laid the groundwork for the discovery of the source of the Nile and was the first white man ever to penetrate the sacred Islamic inner sanctum of Mecca (he would have been torn apart had his disguise been rumbled). He also claimed to be a bastard descendant of Louis XIV. Burton and his literary sidekick, F.F. 'Bunny' Arbuthnot, translated some of India and Persia's great sex texts into English, though their efforts were almost completely banned during Burton's lifetime. Their three most important works were the ancient *Kama Sutra* and the *Ananga Ranga*, both from India, and Persia's *Perfumed Garden*.

The greatest was the *Kama Sutra*, which Burton published privately in 1883, hoping that the book's low profile and small controlled circulation would keep it below the censor's sights. Two years later, he published his translation of the *Ananga Ranga* the same way. At the time, Burton was developing a heroic reputation as a great foreign adventurer, so why did he risk his good name on works that could be derided as smut? Primarily he was obsessed with Eastern culture, and not least its sexual mores. He also hoped that books would help to fund his lifestyle – he was a prolific author and publisher of travel memoirs. There was also a strong streak of sexual evangelism: in the notes to his translation of another Persian book, *The Thousand Nights and a Night*, Burton parodied Western attitudes with the story of a bridegroom who entered the bedchamber to find his bride chloroformed and a note stuck on her pillow: 'Mamma says you're to do what you like.' Burton believed a dose of Eastern salts might help to clear Britain's blockage.

Middle-class Victorian society had developed a surreal talent for perceiving vice, scandal, fornication and depravity wherever it looked. It was obsessed with sex, although this perversely manifested itself as an extremely lurid sense of propriety. Burton's books acted out this repressed fixation by displacing British sexuality to a far-off land where

foreign Johnnies spent their ample spare time copulating all over the place. We still think of the *Kama
Sutra* as proof that everyone beyond Calais lives in a
broiling stew of sex, but in fact the ancient text had
long been out of circulation in its native land.
Burton's helpers struggled to find a complete and
usable copy of the *Kama Sutra* in India. It was the
same story with several other old works of Indian
erotica, but Victorian-era Europeans were sufficiently fascinated to find and revive them. Britain
was even selling the Indians their own sex back.
The most modern Indian posture-book being widely
circulated in India at the time was an English translation of a German compilation of old Indian sex
positions, called the *Kinaesthesia of Love*.

Such convolutions were typical of Burton's life.
He was born in Devon in 1821, a startlingly vivid
redhead. His grandfather had always wanted a red-
haired heir and decided that little Richard should
inherit the family fortune. Grandad was mounting
the steps of his solicitor's, will in hand, when he
dropped dead of a heart attack. Richard did not
inherit. Baby Burton's hair subsequently turned
from red to black. He grew up in France and Italy
before going to Oxford, where he became a notable
fighter and womanizer. He was sent down for
absconding to watch a horse race, which enabled
him to abandon the Church career that his father
had chosen him and to join the Army instead.
Burton bought a commission for £500 in the Bombay
Native Infantry and, on arrival in India, started
learning Hindustani, Gujurati, Persian and the

Hindu religion. Fellow officers called him the White Nigger. He even corralled 40 monkeys together and learnt to imitate their grunts, until he felt they could converse together. His monkey-speak dictionary was not a success, though. Later he studied Islam and attempted the rigorous life of a Sufi.

To learn local Indian customs, he put on long hair and a beard, stained his limbs with henna, and called himself Abdullah of Bushire, a half-Arab. In this guise, he travelled the country offering to sell trinkets in native homes. In Bombay he searched the bazaars for rare books and manuscripts. Around this time, his Army chief, Sir Charles Napier, heard that three houses in Karachi were selling an unspeakable vice – gay sex. Napier needed a spy: Burton was the natural choice. He went undercover into these male brothels, which were staffed by young boys and eunuchs, and found most of the customers to be British officers. His report caused uproar and consigned his Army career to the doldrums. He subsequently contracted cholera and returned to England to recuperate in 1848. But he returned to the foreign fray and in 1861 formally entered the diplomatic service as consul at Equatorial Guinea, and later served in Santos, Brazil, Damascus and Trieste. He wrote books on all these locations.

No one is certain exactly when Burton first met his *Kama Sutra* partner, Forster FitzGerald Arbuthnot (whom he always called Bunny), but by 1853 they were firm friends. Both shared a dream of translating the famous books of the East into English – especially the erotic ones. They believed

they could get away with it if they ensured that
the books were expensive and that only academics
bought them. The pair set up the Kama Shastra
Society in 1882 to publish the books (Kama is the
Hindu love god, Shastra means gospel). It was
merely a front-organization to fend off obscenity
trials. The books purported to be published in
Benares, though really they were printed in Stoke
Newington, in North London.

They planned to publish seven Indian erotic
books, but in the end only the *Kama Sutra* and the
Ananga Ranga appeared. The *Kama Sutra* (its name
can be translated as 'pleasure treatise') is thought to
have been written around AD 300. Virtually nothing
is known about the author, except that his family
name was Vatsyayana and that his own name is
supposed to be Mallinaga or Mrillana. Vatsyayana
says in the introduction that he wrote the *Kama
Sutra* using earlier texts, while studying as a religious student at Benares and contemplating the
divine. The finished work apparently became a
must-read for thousands of Indians, though when
Burton and Arbuthnot began trying to translate it,
no complete copies could be found. Their manuscript was compiled from four incomplete versions
borrowed from Sanskrit libraries around the sub-
continent, along with additions and alterations that
have since been blamed on Burton.

Burton's plan to circumvent British censorship
failed: the authorities promptly banned the book. It
stayed banned for the next 80 years, although short
runs of pirate copies were published. The *Kama*

Sutra's nudge-nudge infamy steadily spread, thanks mainly to the very fact that very few readers ever saw it. For as far as practicalities are concerned, it is possibly the least useful sex manual ever to see printer's ink. The book is written for a narrow, if not non-existent readership: ancient subcontinental equivalents of Hugh Hefner, Indian playboys with little else to do but charm local women into their lavishly appointed homes and then engage in any number of permutations of sex acts from the 529 that legend says are contained in the work. And how do you lure so many women to your bed? The book's advice is to 'carry on an amusing conversation on various subjects'. A few more 'killer chat-up' details might have proved helpful, but then this is all really only an exotic fantasy, an ancient precursor to the sort of 'How to pull a supermodel in 59 seconds' article that men's lifestyle magazines peddle nowadays. Other handy hints include the fact that a married woman might reject your advances if she loves her husband, and that sleeping with ladies who are lepers and lunatics is generally a bad idea. Much of the book's useless information is contained in lists – again, a modern magazine staple, but many of these are particularly bizarre, such as 17 kisses, 16 bites and scratches and 17 slaps and screams. And do you really need to be told that it's a bad idea to bite your partner's eyeball during lovemaking?

The second book Burton and Arbuthnot translated, the *Ananga Ranga of Kalyanamalla* (or *Stage of the Love God*), was written by an Indian poet, Kalyan Mall, and was of no more practical use.

Burton said it was written in about 1450 though other sources say it is far earlier, around 1170. Either way, much of its content was lifted from the *Kama Sutra*. But the work did bring one innovation to the genre – it was the first manual to promise to show you how to 'stay in love with the same lover for the rest of your life'. Kalyan Mall explains: 'The chief reason for the separation between the married couple and the cause which drives the husband to the embraces of strange women, and the wife to the embraces of strange men, is the want of varied pleasures, and the monotony which follows possession.' Burton's evangelism shines through here in a footnote to the *Ananga Ranga's* definition of the woman who can most easily be subdued. It describes her as 'She who has never learnt the real delight of carnal copulation.' Burton's footnote reads, 'This is the case with most English women and a case to be remedied by constant and intelligent study of the *Ananga Ranga* literature.'

Nowadays, it is fashionable to criticize Burton – not least for committing the gross error of being a Victorian and harbouring one or two typically reactionary Victorian attitudes. Wendy Doniger, the American author of a recent *Kama Sutra* translation, accuses him of 'flowery' writing and says he mistranslated sections and obscured the role of women, blatantly altering the text to make them seem more submissive. One glaring example that she quotes describes what a woman should do when her husband is unfaithful. Burton's text says, 'She should not blame him excessively, though she be a little displeased. She should not use abusive language toward him, but rebuke him with conciliatory words.' Doniger argues that the original text says quite the reverse, and should read, 'She scolds him with abusive language when he is alone or among friends.'

The 1970s *Joy of Sex* author, Alex Comfort, also accused Burton of confabulation. He claims that the following description of a handy female trick in the *Ananga Ranga* is actually 'pure Burton' and does not exist in Sanskrit texts: 'She strives to close and constrict the yoni until it holds the penis, as with a finger, opening and shutting at her pleasure and finally acting as the hand of the Gopala-girl who milks the cow. This can only be learnt by long practice. Her husband will then value her above all women, nor would he exchange her for the most beautiful queen in the three worlds.' Whether this addition was in fact made by Burton, Arbuthnot or the Indian pundits who translated the text for them is ultimately unclear. But Burton gets the blame.

Nevertheless, I have stuck with Burton's translations of the *Kama Sutra* and the *Ananga Ranga* in this book, because they are all we really knew in the West for nearly a hundred years, and because they are masterpieces of Victorian strangeness – fossils of our idea that exotic, contortionist copulation exists somewhere 'out there' in a time and place beyond our own narrow rain-sodden lives. These convictions still exist somewhere deep in the British consciousness, making Burton's Indian translations the living coelacanths of sex advice.

Burton has also been accused (oddly) of being a prude. Any such ideas may be banished by reading Chapter One of his translation of the Arabic *Perfumed Garden*. It relates in explicit detail an acrobatic marathon of adulterous sex between the sultan's daughter and the court fool. The book was both a sex manual and a work of erotica, and is believed to have been written in Tunis sometime near the beginning of the sixteenth century. It borrows many of the sexual positions described in earlier Indian texts and throws in some of its own. It also has its own chapters of advice, such as the ideal penis size, penile-enlargement tips (rub with tepid water until red, then anoint with honey and ginger) and herbal cures for impotence, as well as that old favourite: how to seduce women – and how to ditch them afterwards. Burton published the book in 1886, anonymously through the Kama Shastra Society. He did not translate it from Arabic, but used a French translation made before 1850 by an unknown French army officer in Algeria.

Burton also had a hand in *The Priapeia* (1890), an anonymous collection of rude Roman rhymes in praise of the phallic garden-god Priapus, which was translated by L.C. Smithers. Burton's appendix gives explicit explanations for many classical pagan sexual practices and includes a vocabulary of dozens of Latin terms for male and female genitalia, along with essays on classical references to anal and oral sex, bestiality, exotic dancers, masturbation and sex positions. These were so shocking that Burton denied any responsibility, in spite of obvious evidence of his involvement, including several shameless attempts to plug his other books. At the time, Burton was also working on his own original translation of the *Perfumed Garden*. He planned it to be his crowning achievement, a truly comprehensive version (the French version omitted a chapter on homosexuality), complete with all his lifetime's wealth of insights into human sexuality. But, just as his life had started with a mishap, it ended with one: Burton died in 1890 just before he was to publish the new book. Lady Isabel Burton (with whom he shared a strangely sexless marriage) examined the manuscript, along with his reputedly pornographic travel journals, and thought it all way too strong. She burned his wealth of papers, even though she had been offered six thousand guineas for them.

Despite all his achievements as a great Victorian explorer, the sex books meant that Burton was considered unfit to be buried in Westminster Abbey alongside Dr Livingstone. He lies instead at Mortlake Cemetery in south-west London. Isabel moved to a cottage overlooking her husband's tomb before dying six years later. The *Kama Sutra* remained banned in Britain until 1963.

Positions, Everybody

Fish gobbling?

Mawangdui medical manuscripts (200–300 BC)

Tiger roving (rear entry on all fours)
Cicada clinging (rear entry, woman lying face down)
Measuring worm (both parties bending and
    stretching)
Gibbon grabbing (woman's feet over man's
    shoulders)
Rabbit bolting (woman on top, facing his feet)
Fish gobbling (woman on top)

Pick your prettiest posture

Ovid's poem, *Ars Amatoria*
(*The Art of Love*) (c. I BC)

Let every woman, then, learn to know herself,
    and to enter upon love's battle in the pose
    best suited to her charms
If a woman has a lovely face, let her lie upon
    her back
If she prides herself upon her hips, let her
    display them to best advantage
Melanion bore Atlanta's legs upon his
    shoulders; if your legs are as beautiful as
    hers, put them in the same position
If you are short, go on top
A woman who is conspicuously tall should
    kneel with her head turned slightly sideways

If your thighs are still lovely with the charm of
   youth, if your bosom is without flaw, lie across
   your bed and think it not a shame to let your
   hair float unbraided about your shoulders
If the labours of childbirth have left their mark
   upon you, then turn your back to the action.
   Love has a thousand postures; the simplest and
   the least fatiguing is to lie on your right side
Don't let the light in your bedroom be too
   bright; there are many things about a woman
   that are best seen in the dimness of twilight

Stick to the missionary

Artemidoros of Daldis, itinerant
Greco-Roman dream analyst and sex guru (2 BC)

It is not advantageous to employ many and various
positions ... Other positions are human inventions
prompted by insolence, dissipation and debauchery.
The fact that the frontal position alone is taught by
nature is clear from other animals. All species
employ some regular position and do not alter it,
because they follow the rationale of nature.

For instance, some mount from behind (horse, ass,
goat, cow, deer and some other four-footed animals),
some first bring their mouths together (vipers, doves,
weasels), some are very quick (sparrows). Some, by
the weight of their mounting, force the females into
a sitting position (all birds), some do not even
approach each other – the females gather up all the
seeds emitted by the males (fish).

New Year's hammock

From the 16th-century Arabic book, *The Old Man Young Again*, translated by Charles Carrington (1898)

The man and the woman sit in a swinging hammock on New Year's Day, the woman placing herself on the man's lap, over his penis, which is standing. They then take hold of one another, she placing her two legs against his two sides, and set the swinging hammock in motion. And thus when the hammock goes on one side he comes out of her, and when it goes to the other side he goes into her, and so they go on swiving without inconvenience or tire, but with endearment and tender braying, till depletion comes to both of them. This is called the Congress of the New Year's Hammock.

Splitting the coconut

Top postures from the Javanese *Serat Candraning Wanita* (*Book of Descriptions of Women*) – traditional folklore

Snake-like: both partners lying on their sides, face to face
Crocodile: the missionary
Animal: both partners kneeling
Monkey takes care of its child: standing up*
Splitting open a coconut: woman on top
Deer with branched horns: woman on her back with both legs raised

*Beware: the resulting child will suffer from a pathological compulsion to urinate frequently.

The 'cross-dresser'

Gilbert Oakley, *Sane and Sensual Sex* (1963)

Some wives prefer to take the active position from time to time. They like to have the man underneath and to go through the vigorous, masculine movements until mutual orgasm is achieved. If the wise husband permits this, he is not being disloyal to his sex, demeaning himself or making himself female by playing the feminine role. He is giving his wife the satisfaction of working off the masculine side of her nature from time to time, in just the same way as he might like to work off the feminine side to his nature by wearing girls' undies.

First, push her head down her knickers

Perfumed Garden of Sheik Nefzaoui (16th century), translated into English by Sir Richard F. Burton

The summersault: woman wears knickers around her ankles, then puts her head between her feet, so it's caught in her knickers. Man, seizes her legs, pushes her on her back, making her summersault, then takes her from on top

Frog fashion: woman on back with heels against buttocks and knees under man's armpits

The screw of Archimedes: woman on top, taking her weight on her hands so that bellies don't touch

Reciprocal sight of the posteriors: man lies on back, woman mounts with her back to him. He raises his feet over her back, she bends her head down and looks backwards.

Never standing up ... or sitting down

Nicholas Venette, *The Mysteries of Conjugal Love Reveald* (1703)

Nature teaches both sexes such postures as are allowable and contribute to generation, and experience teaches such as are forbidden and destructive to health. The genital parts of men are not contrived to caress standing; our health receiving great inconveniences in a posture so opposite to generation; for all the nervous parts being strained, are put to pain.

The eyes are dazzled, and head swims, the backbone suffers, the knees tremble and the legs seem to yield to the weight of the whole body. In short, it is the spring and source of all our weakness, gouts and rheumatisms. Nor is a sitting posture becoming an orderly love, it being difficult for the parts to join and the seed to be received ...

Man, according to the laws of nature, ought to have empire over the woman, and being counted lord of all creatures, is very base to submit in love exploits. It is beneath his prerogative to yield to the caprices of a woman abandoned to such lewd tricks.

Or upside-down

Jesuit Thomas Sanchez,
De Sancto Matrimonio (early 16th century)

It is a mortal sin for a husband and wife to have intercourse with the normal position reversed, because it makes the woman active which, as anyone can see, Nature must abhor. Furthermore, according to certain authorities the Flood was caused by the vile custom of women mounting upon men in the sexual act.

Upside-down (again)

Perfumed Garden of Sheik Nefzaoui (16th century),
translated into English by Sir Richard F. Burton

Do not let the woman perform the act of coition mounted upon you, for fear that in that position some drops of her seminal fluid might enter the canal of your penis and cause a sharp urethritis.

- or standing up (again)

Coition if performed standing affects the knee-joints and brings about nervous shiverings; and if performed sideways will predispose your system for gout and sciatica, which resides chiefly in the hip joint.

Hot position tip

Kama Sutra of Vatsyayana (3rd century),
translated by Sir Richard F. Burton and F.F. Arbuthnot (1883)

Practise all these different ways of lying down, sitting, and standing, in water, because it is easier to do so there. (Look out for the lifeguard.)

Man-lion or creeper cling?

Ratimanjari of Jayadeva (*The Posy of Love*)
(India, *c.* 16th century)

The creeper cling (man wraps woman with arms and legs)

Half casket (man on knees holds woman's feet aloft and massages her breasts)

The thunderbolt (man violently parts woman's feet and batters her with penis)

The wave (man holds woman's feet to his chest and penetrates her at his leisure)

Man-lion (man presses woman's feet together, violently penetrates her and embraces tightly)

The warlock (man seizes woman's thighs, strikes her with hands and takes her with extreme violence).

But whatever you do, stay pliable

Marie Stopes, *Married Love* (1918)

A pair should, impelled by the great wave of feeling within them, be as pliable as the sea-plants moved by the rushing tides, and they should discover for themselves which of the innumerable possible positions of equilibrium results in the greatest mutual satisfaction. In this matter, as in so many others of the more intimate phases of sex-life, there should not harden a routine, but the body should become at the service of intense feeling a keen and pliable instrument.

Or else ...

Lyman B. Sperry, *Confidential Talks with Husband and Wife: a book of information and advice for the married and marriageable* (1900)

Any position that is painful to the wife should be religiously avoided.

Read your woman in bed

Mawangdui medical manuscripts (200–300 BC)

A woman's posture will tell you how to thrust:

When she clasps hands, she wants her abdomen
   pressed

When she extends her elbows, she wants her
   upper vagina rubbed

When she straightens heels, entry is
   insufficiently deep

When she raises her flanks, she wants her walls
   rubbed

When she raises her torso, she wants the lower
   part rubbed

When she crosses her thighs, penetration is
   excessive

When she shakes, she wants the man to
   continue holding for long time

Twelve

MR SEX IN SANDALS

Until this point in modern history, gay sex was the ultimate unspeakable where love manuals were concerned.

It took a wealthy Cambridge graduate turned anarcho-socialist sandal-maker to break the taboo, and even then he had a false start.

Edward Carpenter has been called the gay godfather of the British left, and in 1929 was grovellingly described by the Labour MP Fenner Brockway as having 'head and features of extraordinary beauty, his face a chiselled statue'. Brockway added, 'One admired him and loved him at once.' Carpenter's vision of an ideal socialist life provided an inspiration for the founders of the Independent Labour Party. He foresaw a world where men and women would be bound together by the force of love, rather than by work or economics. He was an active Victorian politician who spent much of his time giving public lectures, but nevertheless he found it surprisingly easy to live in an open gay relationship with his lover, George Merrill, an unemployed man he met on a train in 1889.

When Carpenter wrote his marriage guide, *Love's Coming of Age*, it included the first chapter positively to approve of gay sex in a post-Classical manual: even the revolutionary likes of Drysdale and Carlile had condemned homosexuality as obscene. But the chapter was taken out before the book was typeset in 1896. He and his publishers got cold feet, which was perfectly understandable given that the trial of Oscar Wilde the previous year had once again cast the jailer's shadow over open gay expression. It was another ten years before the gay chapter was added, by which time the book had become a highly influential guide to sexual conduct.

Carpenter was virulently opposed to conventional marriage, saying it turned women into serfs and men into cheats. Instead he argued for more open, or at least 'less prettily exclusive', relationships. At the same time, however, he criticized promiscuity. Not only were his ethics a bit confused, but his predictions that humankind would adopt Karezza (a form of Tantric sex, see page 142) as contraception, and that a communist society would liberate women from housework, were rather wide of the mark.

Ultimately, Carpenter and his beardy-weirdy good intentions fell victim to a purge by Labour modernizers. His advanced ideas clashed with the responsible fit-to-govern image that the Labour Party wanted to foster between the two world wars, and he was quietly dropped from favour. George Orwell apparently had Carpenter in mind in *The Road to Wigan Pier* when he condemned the idiot socialist cliché of a 'fruit-juice drinker, nudist, sandal wearer and sex maniac'.

Corporal Funishment

Mutual repulsion and hatred 'quite normal'

Theodoor Hendrik Van de Velde, *Ideal Marriage,
Its Physiology and Technique* (1928)

Love bites can be given out of concentrated sexual hatred: not out of any degree of sexual love. Only a very superficial observer can miss the primitive repulsion and antagonism between the sexes which is as real as and more permanent than the attraction. The attraction may, and often does, prevail for a time; but the antipathy is there and its expression is much wider and often quite as vigorous.

Underneath love there always lies in wait hatred. And surely this is one of the profoundest causes of the tragedy of humanity. It is the possibility that gives such a sinister suggestion to the love-bite – and to the triumphant slap with the open hand on the buttocks which many a man either gives his partner, or feels an impulse to give her, at the conclusion of coitus. For these manifestations are quite 'normal'.

How to hit someone - and how to say ouch!

Kama Sutra of Vatsyayana (3rd century),
translated by Sir Richard F. Burton and F.F. Arbuthnot (1883)

Sex can be compared to a quarrel, on account of the contrarieties of love and its tendency to cause rows. The place of striking with passion is the body, and on the body the special places are:

The shoulders
The head
The space between the breasts
The back
The middle part of the body
The sides

Four kinds of strike:
With the back of the hand
With the fingers a little contracted
With the fist
With the open palm of the hand

Eight types of yelp:
On account of its causing pain, striking gives rise to the hissing sound, which is of various kinds, and to the eight kinds of crying:

The sound Hin
The thundering sound
The cooing sound
The weeping sound
The sound Phut
The sound Phât
The sound Sût
The sound Plât

Blows with the fist should be given on the back of the woman while she is sitting on the lap of the man, and she should give blows in return, abusing the man as if she were angry, and making the cooing and the weeping sounds. While the woman is engaged in congress the space between the breasts should be struck with the back of the hand, slowly at first, and then proportionately to the increasing excitement, until the end.

At this time the sounds Hin and others may be made, alternately or optionally, according to habit. When the man, making the sound Phât, strikes the woman on the head, with the fingers of his hand a little contracted, it is called Prasritaka, which means striking with the fingers of the hand a little contracted. In this case the appropriate sounds are the cooing sound, the sound Phât and the sound Phut in the interior of the mouth, and at the end of congress the sighing and weeping sounds.

The sound Phât is an imitation of the sound of a bamboo being split, while the sound Phut is like the sound made by something falling into water. At all times when kissing and such like things are begun, the woman should give a reply with a hissing sound. During the excitement when the woman is not accustomed to striking, she continually utters words expressive of prohibition, sufficiently, or desire of liberation, as well as the words 'father', 'mother', intermingled with the sighing, weeping and thundering sounds.

Towards the conclusion of the congress, the breasts, the middle parts, and sides of the woman should be pressed with the open palms of the hand, with some force, until the end of it, and then sounds like those of the quail or the goose should be made.

'You're killing me!' And other shouts

Koka Shastra (*The Scripture of Koka*),
by the Indian poet Kokkoka (12th century)

Stop!
Harder!
Go on!
Don't kill me!
No!

(Hope you've got thick party walls.)

Playful little smacks

Rennie MacAndrew, *Life Long Love:*
healthy sex and marriage (1928)

No reasonable means of stimulation which leads up
to and culminates in intercourse is a perversion,
providing nothing other than the two bodies is used ...
Of course the man who gets pleasure by beating his
wife is deviating from normal, but mutual and playful
little smacks could not be called abnormal.

How to scratch and bite

Kama Sutra of Vatsyayana (3rd century),
translated by Sir Richard F. Burton and F.F. Arbuthnot (1883)

Scratching school

Scratches are named after the marks they produce:

> Half moon (simple curved nail indent on neck
> or breasts)
> Circle (two indents together on neck or breasts)
> Line (it's a line)
> Tiger's nail or claw (curved line on breast)
> Peacock's foot (all five nails scratching the breast
> – 'this requires great skill to do it properly')
> The jump of a hare (five marks with the nails are
> made close to one another near the nipple)
> The leaf of a blue lotus (leaf-shaped mark on
> the breast or on the hips)

– and where to scratch:

The places that are to be pressed with the nails are as follows: the armpit, the throat, the breasts, the lips, the jaghana, or middle parts of the body, and the thighs. When the impetuosity of passion is excessive, the places need not be considered.

The love of a woman who sees the marks of nails on the private parts of her body, even though they are old and almost worn out, becomes again fresh and new. Even when a stranger sees at a distance a young woman with the marks of nails on her breast, he is filled with love and respect for her.

A man who carries the marks of nails and teeth on some parts of his body influences the mind of a woman. In short, nothing tends to increase love so much as the effects of marking with the nails, and biting.

How to bite (NB - avoid the eyes)

All the places that can be kissed are also the places that can be bitten, except the upper lip, the interior of the mouth, and the eyes.

The qualities of good teeth are as follows: they should be equal, possessed of a pleasing brightness, capable of being coloured, of proper proportions, unbroken, and with sharp ends.

The defects of teeth on the other hand are that they are blunt, protruding from the gums, rough, soft, large, and loosely set.

The following are the different kinds of biting:

The hidden bite
The swollen bite
The point
The line of points
The coral and the jewel
The line of jewels
The broken cloud
The biting of the boar

The biting, which is shown only by the excessive redness of the skin that is bitten, is called the 'hidden bite'.

When the skin is pressed down on both sides, it is called the 'swollen bite'.

When a small portion of the skin is bitten with two teeth only, it is called the 'point'.

When such small portions of the skin are bitten with all the teeth, it is called the 'line of points'.

The biting, which is done by bringing together the teeth and the lips, is called the 'coral and the jewel'. The lip is the coral, and the teeth the jewel.

When biting is done with all the teeth, it is called the 'line of jewels'.

The biting, which consists of unequal risings in a circle, and which comes from the space between the teeth, is called the 'broken cloud'. This is impressed on the breasts.

The biting, which consists of many broad rows of marks near to one another, and with red intervals, is called the 'biting of a boar'. This is impressed on the breasts and the shoulders; and these two last modes of biting are peculiar to persons of intense passion.

The lower lip is the place on which the 'hidden bite', the 'swollen bite', and the 'point' are made; again the 'swollen bite' and the 'coral and the jewel' bite are done on the cheek. Kissing, pressing with the nails, and biting are the ornaments of the left cheek, and when the word cheek is used it is to be understood as the left cheek.

Both the 'line of points' and the 'line of jewels' are to be impressed on the throat, the armpit, and the joints of the thighs; but the 'line of points' alone is to be impressed on the forehead and the thighs.

The marking with the nails, and the biting of the following things - an ornament of the forehead, an ear ornament, a bunch of flowers, a betel leaf, or a tamala leaf, which are worn by, or belong to the woman that is beloved - are signs of the desire of enjoyment.

When a man bites a woman forcibly, she should angrily do the same to him with double force. Thus a 'point' should be returned with a 'line of points', and a 'line of points' with a 'broken cloud', and if she be excessively chafed, she should at once begin a love quarrel with him.

Have you got all that?

Thirteen

AMERICAN DUTY

The first sex manual to hit American shores was most probably Aristotle's *Masterpiece*, which was initially imported from Britain in the early 1700s.

The first American edition was printed in 1766, as a 'pack book' to be sold by peddlers. Around 50 editions followed and its popularity in the United States stretched from colonial times to the twentieth century. Masturbation paranoia was an early invader, too. Marten's *Onania* travelled to the American colonies in 1724 and Samuel-Auguste Tissot's *L'Onanisme* followed a few decades after. Fear of sex – and in particular, self-abuse – steadily grew into an all-American bogeyman. From around 1830 onwards, books and pamphlets describing the terrible effects of sexual indulgence became more common and increasingly strident.

A legion of nineteenth-century quacks and amateurs joined this crusade to keep the American Dream dry. Among the curious cohort was the former clergyman Sylvester Graham, whose lust-defeating wholewheat flour produced the original

Graham Cracker. In 1834, his *Lecture to Young Men on Chastity* declared that sex leads to insanity and that every ejaculation shortens life expectancy – the latter idea being a strange echo of the 'sexual cultivation' practices promoted by ancient Chinese texts. Graham added that excessive carnal exercise would cause indigestion, headache, feebleness of circulation, consumption, spinal disease, epilepsy, insanity and early death of offspring, among other things. He thought men should remain virgins until aged 30 and subsequently should make love only once a month – and not at all if they were sickly.

To control the evils of lust, Graham prescribed a special vegetarian diet, the centrepiece of which was Graham bread, made from wholewheat flour. Graham Crackers, which he invented in 1829, were another manifestation of his campaign for unstimulating food. In his 1849 *Lectures on the Science of Human Life*, he warned that pastries, with the exception of fruit pies, were 'among the most pernicious articles of human ailment'. Graham attracted a fair number of followers, who opened Graham boarding houses in New York and Boston where his diet was strictly observed. But most people regarded him as a nut. He was assaulted by mobs on at least three occasions, once by butchers and bakers who thought he was going to drive them out of business. Predictably perhaps, he ended up going crackers, becoming increasingly strange and aloof and alienating even his closest admirers. He gave up lecturing in 1839 and his life ended in obscurity.

Far more popular was the Seventh-day Adventist prophet Ellen G. White. In 1864, she devoted her first book on health reform, *Appeal to Mothers*, entirely to warning Adventist parents of the dire consequences of self-abuse. But what would White, a poorly educated farmer's daughter, know about medical science? In the book, she claimed her knowledge came from visions sent to her from heaven: 'The state of our world was presented before me, and my attention was especially called to the youth of our time. Everywhere I looked, I saw imbecility, dwarfed forms, crippled limbs, misshapen heads, and deformity of every description. Sins and crimes, and the violation of nature's laws, were shown me as the causes of this accumulation of human woe and suffering. I saw such degradation and vile practices.' Critics claimed, however, that she had merely copied out swathes of work from other contemporary anti-masturbatory books.

Frederick Hollick: Sexual Medicine

Not all American advice was quite so negative. One of the most popular lecturers and authors of the time was Frederick Hollick, a self-appointed expert from Philadelphia who in 1844 began lecturing in New York City and soon toured around much of America, attracting large crowds. Why so popular? It helped that his talks were tinged with pornography. His cannabis aphrodisiacs can't have hindered business either. Hollick's sexual medicine shows could not use naked women, so he used the next best thing, papier-mâché anatomical models which were allegedly made in Paris. These he used to present risqué titbits under the guise of scientific edification. The models were so natural they caused a sensation and inspired many imitators.

Hollick, naturally enough, had also climbed aboard the anti-onanist bandwagon. And why not? By now it was clear that masturbation was the one burning guilt common to all clean-living, Calvinist soul-searching Americans. He started publishing his lectures in 1845, and in his early book, *The Male Generative Organs in Health and Disease, from Infancy to Old Age*, used figures from annual reports of the Massachusetts State Lunatic Asylum to 'prove' that white-collar work causes self-abuse far more than healthy outdoor labour. Hollick recognized that women should orgasm – but only with men. Persistent female onanists might need their clitorises removed, he said.

In 1846 he faced criminal charges of obscene libel. Prosecutors argued that his lectures were salacious rather than informative and contained very little science. But Hollick had the people behind him: his loyal listeners and readers mobilized through the letters pages of daily newspapers to accuse the medical profession of trying to build a monopoly of health information. They also demanded the right to learn about sex and contraception. Hollick beat the rap.

His other achievement was to help America to get stoned, as part of his mail-order business that also offered a 'superior' brand of condoms for $9 and a syphilis preventative for $10. He grew the grass himself and sold it as a love potion, claiming that his research revealed the central ingredient in all known aphrodisiacs and exhilarants was good old cannabis. In one advert, he told potential customers: 'The true aphrodisiac, as I compound it, acts upon the brain and nervous system, not as a stimulant, but as a tonic and nutritive agent, thus sustaining its power and the power of the sexual organs also, which is entirely dependent upon the nervous power.' He added, 'A gentleman can keep it in his vest pocket without any fear of detection from smell, or appearance. It will go anywhere by post, with perfect safety, and in such a form that no one through whose hands it passes would ever suspect its nature, or that it is anything peculiar.' How very handy.

Monkey Business? It's for Kids

Didn't anyone notice anything peculiar about *Sammy Tubbs, the Boy Doctor, and Sponsie, the Troublesome Monkey*? Because ironically, this voluminous children's book turned out to be one of the most explicit sex guides of the era, diagrams and all – and featured in its 1,200 pages a taboo-breaking bout of interracial love as well.

Sammy Tubbs was written in 1874 and starred Tubbs, 12-year-old son of freed slaves and his sidekick monkey called Sponsie. It featured the world's first anatomically explicit sex education published for pre-adolescent children. The hero, Tubbs, is the protégé of a Manhattan doctor Samuel Hubbs, who moulds the young black boy into a fully qualified medic. Together, through four volumes, they explore the ins and outs of the human body – muscles, circulation, digestion and the nervous system. To keep things entertaining, Sponsie acts the troublesome monkey. But in volume five, things take a distinctly gynaecological tone – literally in the case of one illustration, which oddly shows a vagina with a tiny musical note peeping out. The volume's cover carries the warning: 'Book for Private Reading'. This sex-education section succeeded in being both forthright and graphic, drawing and describing everything a child might want to know – and perhaps more. The author had thoughtfully provided an escape route for parents who found it all too much: one set of particularly strong pictures is printed on page '180 and a half' – so that sensitive mums and dads could tear out the drawings without their children ever noticing anything was missing.

Sammy Tubbs's author was the health crusader, mail-order magnate, newspaper publisher and Unitarian agnostic Dr Edward Bliss Foote. He was a typical Victorian health-maniac, and his book contains many of contemporary America's obsessions – lectures against tight-fitting clothes, tobacco and alcohol, and passages promoting phrenology and animal magnetism. He had been an early contraceptive entrepreneur and manufactured a one-size-fits-all womb veil, a sort of Dutch cap, in the 1860s and sold it for $6 at clinics and through mail order, until the ultra-repressive Comstock Laws banned the manufacture and sale of contraceptives and the sending of contraceptive information through the post.

Foote fell foul of the federal Comstock Law in 1874, and was fined $3,500 for mailing an educational pamphlet advocating the right of families to limit their size through 'contraceptics', called *Confidential Pamphlet for the Married; words in pearl for married people only*. (Comstock's other high-profile victims, Ida Craddock and Margaret Sanger, feature on pages 146 and 217.) But Foote had better luck with his *Medical Common Sense*, which sold a quarter of a million copies despite including information on using douching as a contraceptive method.

He was a race campaigner as well. Tubbs would now be labelled a 'positive racial role model'; in the story he becomes a local medical practitioner and health lecturer, addressing halls packed with black and white women. And Tubbs has a white girlfriend, Julia, who, just to nail the message firmly home, is the daughter of a cotton broker. Foote advocated interracial relationships on the eugenic grounds of avoiding racial inbreeding. Such were his convictions that he even included a picture of Sammy and Julia kissing – possibly the first positive illustration of an interracial kiss in 19th-century American fiction.

J.H. Kellogg: Cereal Sex Killer

Far less healthy back then was a name now associated with wakey-wakey sunshine breakfast-time – John Harvey Kellogg, MD, the originator of cornflakes and the author of the 1877 guide *Plain Facts about Sexual Life*.

J.H. Kellogg was about as qualified to compose a sex guide as the Dalai Lama is to write books on hand-to-hand combat. Not only was Kellogg a virgin, but he believed sex was debilitating. He never consummated his own marriage and preferred instead to receive an enema from an orderly every morning after breakfast – which beats trying to clip a small plastic toy together. The radical advocate of vegetarianism spent his honeymoon writing his *Plain Facts* as a treatise on the evils of sexuality. Yet again, it obsessed about the potential dangers of self-abuse. The book proved highly popular in the late 1800s, scaring secret self-pleasurers with dire warnings of persistent headaches, indigestion, weakness of the back and knees, disturbed circulation, dimness of vision and loss of appetite – all ailments that could be developed psychosomatically, given with the right blend of guilt and fear.

Losing semen more than once a month – even in marital relations – should cause alarm, warned Kellogg. 'The seminal fluid is the most vitalized of all the fluids of the body, and that its rapid production is at the expense of a lost exhaustive effort on the part of the vital forces, is well attested by all physiologists.' To save the world, he invented corn-flakes as one part of a diet that he felt would lessen the sex drive. Like Graham, he thought that tasty food was the Devil's work. 'Exciting stimulants and condiments weaken and irritate nerves, and derange the circulation,' he wrote in *Plain Facts*. 'Thus, indirectly they affect the sexual system, which suffers through sympathy with the other organs. But a more direct injury is done. Flesh, condiments, eggs, tea, coffee, chocolate, and all stimulants have a powerful influence directly upon the reproductive organs. They increase the local supply of blood; and through nervous sympathy with the brain, the passions are aroused.'

There were many other ways your mouth could get you into trouble, he wrote: 'Overeating, eating between meals, hasty eating, eating indigestible articles of food, ices, late suppers, etc., react upon the sexual organs with the utmost certainty. Any disturbance of the digestive function deteriorates the quality of the blood. Poor blood, filled with crude, poorly digested food, is irritating to the nervous system, and especially to those extremely delicate nerves which govern the reproductive function. Irritation provokes congestion; congestion excites sexual desires; excited passions increase the local disturbance.'

Smoking was out, too: 'The lecherous day-dreams in which many smokers indulge, are a species of fornication for which even a brute ought to blush, if such a crime were possible for a brute. The mental libertine does not confine himself to the women of the town. In the foulness of his imagination, he invades the sanctity of virtue wherever his erotic fancy leads him.' No wonder people find it so hard to give up.

Kellogg's best-selling rant encouraged a further surge of anti-onanist propaganda, including *Dr Henry Guernsey's Plain Talks on Avoided Subjects*, which was first published in 1882 and reprinted four times before a revised edition came out in 1915. The paranoia spread to ever younger ages: Guernsey warned parents to keep an eye on their children's play, in case it accidentally prompted sexual impressions by 'allowing them to repose playfully on their belly, to slide down banisters or to go too long without urinating'.

Banister-sliding is, he warned, particularly dangerous, as it can lead to 'inveterate masturbation', which in turn 'is repeated time after time until the degrading and destructive (morally and physically so) habit is confirmed. As a result the boy grows thin, pale, morose and passionate; then weak, indolent and indifferent; his digestion becomes impaired, his sleep short, disturbed and broken; he sometimes becomes epileptic or falls into a state of marasmus; in any case he is in great danger of being totally ruined forever.'

His Masturbator's Voice: the Rants of Sylvanus Stall

Why stop at books when a new gadget is at hand? Sylvanus Stall was a Lutheran pastor, the associate editor of *The Lutheran Observer* and author of such hot reads as 1880's *How to Pay Church Debts and How to Keep Churches Out of Debt*. He might have stuck with the episcopal-funding genre had he not hit on a way of using the power of America's inventiveness to keep its children's hands out of their pockets.

In 1905, he used the very latest technology to preach his dictum, 'No boy can toy with exposed portions of his reproductive system without finally suffering very serious consequences.' He marketed one of the first ever talking books. It could be purchased as a set of 24 wax cylinders. In them Sylvanus gives 'little Harry' a series of sermonizing lectures guaranteed to screw him up for the rest of his life. And there must have been plenty of poor little Harrys out there. Stall's work featured numerous endorsements from prominent Americans and went into scores of editions and many languages.

It is Stall's solemn duty to warn against the dangers, once again, of solitary vice – a pleasurable sensation boys discover at a very early age by climbing trees, riding on horseback, having itchy genitals or, once again, sliding down banisters. Or some boys' nurses might, says Dr Stall, have given them a quick helping hand 'for the purpose of diverting their thoughts, so that they will not cry, or in order that they may be quieted when put to bed and soon fall asleep'. What made him think that? Stall also relates a tale of onanistic mischief which of course ends badly, with the poor young victim suffering 'a spasm of the nerves, terminating for the time all pleasure, and leaving the nerves as wasted and depleted as the body of a person whose entire physical system has been brought under the influence of a spasm'.

And in case one spasm were not enough to put you off, Stall warns: 'If such shocks are repeated, or long continued, the entire nervous system will eventually become shattered and ruined beyond all hope of complete recovery. The health gradually declines. The eyes lose their lustre. The skin becomes sallow. The muscles become flabby. There is an unnatural languor. Every little effort is followed by weariness. There is a great indifference to exertion. Work becomes distasteful and irksome. He complains of pain in the back; of headache and dizziness. The hands become cold and clammy. The digestion becomes poor, and appetite fitful. The heart palpitates. He sits in a stooping position, becomes hollow-chested, and the entire body, instead of enlarging into a strong, manly frame, becomes wasted, and many signs give promise of early decline and death.'

Just Don't: Religious Bans and Priestly Punishments

Sex (ad)vice

Penitential of Theodore of Tarsus, the Archbishop of Canterbury (c. 668–690)

If anyone commits fornication with a virgin he shall do penance for one year. If with a married woman, he shall do penance for four years, two of these entire and in the other two during the three 40-day fasting periods [before Easter, before Christmas and after Pentecost] and three days a week.

He who often commits fornication with a man or with a beast should do penance for ten years.

He who defiles himself, 40 days.

He who desires to commit fornication, but is not able, shall do penance for 40 or 20 days.

As for boys who mutually engage in vice, they should be whipped.

If a woman practises vice with a woman, she shall do penance for three years.

If she practises solitary vice, she shall do penance for the same period.

Whoever has emitted semen in the mouth shall do penance for seven years. This is the worst of evils.

If one commits fornication with his mother, he shall do penance for 15 years and never change clothes except on Sundays.

He who commits fornication with his sister shall do penance for 15 years in the way which is stated above of his mother.

If a brother commits fornication with a natural brother, he shall abstain from all kinds of flesh for 15 years.

If a mother imitates acts of fornication with her little son, she shall abstain from flesh for three years and fast one day in the week.

He who amuses himself with libidinous imagination shall do penance until the imagination is overcome.

He who has intercourse [with his wife] on the Lord's day shall seek pardon from God and do penance for one or two or three days.

If a man has intercourse with his wife from behind, he shall do penance for 40 days for the first time.

If he has intercourse in the rear, he ought to do penance as one who offends with animals.

A husband who sleeps with his wife shall wash himself before he goes into a church.

A husband ought not to see his wife nude.

If a man and a woman have united in marriage, and afterward the woman says of the man that he is impotent, if anyone can prove that this is true, she may take another husband.

Punishments for priests

If a priest is polluted in touching or kissing a woman he shall do penance for 40 days.

If a presbyter is polluted through masturbation,
he shall fast for three weeks.
A holy monk or holy virgin who commits
fornication shall do penance for seven years.

The higher you go, the deeper you fall

Peter Damian, *Liber Gomorrhianus* (c. 1048–54)

Four types of this form of criminal wickedness can
be distinguished in an effort to show you the totality
of the whole matter in an orderly way: some sin with
themselves alone [masturbation]; some by the hands
of others [mutual masturbation]; others between the
thighs [interfemoral intercourse]; and finally, others
commit the complete act against nature [anal inter-
course].

The ascending gradation among these is such that
the last mentioned are judged to be more serious
than the preceding. Indeed a greater penance is
imposed on those who sin with others than those
who defile only themselves; and those who complete
the act are to be judged more severely than those

who are defiled through femoral fornication. The devil's artful fraud devises these degrees of falling into ruin such that the higher the level the unfortunate soul reaches in them, the deeper they sink in the depths of hell's pit.

How to say, 'No thank you'

St Paul, *I Corinthians, 7:5*

Do not deprive one another except perhaps by agreement for a set time, to devote yourselves to prayer, and then come together again, so that Satan may not tempt thou because of your lack of self-control.

Six legit reasons for a wife to refuse sex

Spanish Jesuit Bartolomeo de Medina's
brief instructions for confessors (*c.* 1581)

If the marriage has not yet been consummated and she decides to become a nun

If the husband has committed adultery

If her life or health is in danger

If the husband requests sex at a sacred place or public location

If the sex act involves ejaculation outside the vagina

If the husband has taken a vow of chastity, but now wants to lapse

It's OK to pull out of a prostitute

De Sancto Matrimonio, by Jesuit Thomas Sanchez
(early 16th century)

If, when engaged in sex with a whore, a man withdraws before ejaculation, he is considered to have repented and not sinned against God's laws.

Fast seducers get off lightly

Sefer Hassidim (*Ashkenazi Jewish Book*)
(13th century)

An adulterer who is prepared to repent should sit in an icy river for the time that elapsed from the moment he first spoke to the woman until he consummated the affair. If it is summer, he should instead sit on an ant hill.

Fourteen

SEXUAL PIONEERS

A product of the great outdoors, Alice Stockham
wanted sex to last for ever, as an American
pioneer of tantric sex.

Over the past century, tantra has become, like the
Kama Sutra, a Western byword for convoluted
Oriental practices – weird sex practised by mystic
Easterners and the occasional Western rock star
anxious to reassure the world of their continued
virility. In its native India, tantra covers a gamut of
sexual yoga practices, but in the West it has come to
mean having sex for hours, if not days, without the
man ejaculating – a sort of penile self-anaesthetic
that is claimed to transport practitioners to spiritual
ecstasy. Once again, we hear an echo of those first
Chinese love guides.

The practice only became widely known in the
West during the 19th century, with a sudden and
apparently coincidental burst of interest from
several esoteric writers. Perhaps it was sexual
synchronicity: each pioneer was sure that they had
discovered it by themselves. And each gave it their
own title, such as 'Male Continence', 'Magnetation',

'The Better Way' and 'Zugassent's Discovery'. Alice Bunker Stockham, however, was the only one to travel to India to study Hindu tantric sex for herself. In 1896, she published her own feminist version of orgasmless sex and called it 'karezza' – Italian for caress.

Stockham's background could qualify her to be the Calamity Jane of strange contraception. She was born in 1833 in the old Wild West of Michigan, where home was a log cabin and the neighbours were Native American tribespeople. She grew up a Quaker and paid her way through high school with manual labour. At the age of 20, she got into Cincinnati's Eclectic College to study medicine and was among the first five women in America to qualify as a medical doctor. She specialized in obstetrics and gynaecology and became an activist in women's and children's rights. She was also a homoeopath, a suffragette and a trance medium. When the first tantra books were translated into English, Stockham wanted to know more and travelled to Southern India, visiting a hereditary female caste of warriors on the Malabar Coast. The Nayar women were wise, educated, and all property descended through them. They ran businesses, chose their own (multiple) husbands, and were tagged the 'free women of India'. They also knew a few things about spiritual sex.

Classic Indian tantra casts women as vessels for men to use to generate their spiritual energy. But Stockham's female-friendly version claimed that both men and women could benefit from conserving and exchanging their sexual essences. By holding it all back, the couple could rev themselves up into sexually charged spiritual dynamos whose healthful vigour could drive creative and spiritual achievements that would change the world, such as great inventions and beautiful works of art.

What's more, the system could also sort out your domestic life: 'Men who are borne down with sorrow because their wives are nervous, feeble and irritable, have it in their power, through karezza, to restore the radiant hue of health to the faces of their loved ones, strength and elasticity to their steps and harmonious action to every part of their bodies,' promised Stockham. 'By manifestation of tenderness and endearment, the husband may develop a response in the wife through her love nature, which thrills every fibre into action and radiates tonic to every nerve ... The common daily sarcasms of married people are at an end, the unseemly quarrels have no beginnings and the divorce courts are cheated of their records.' Some upside. And the downside of indulging in regular coital orgasms is, she warned, 'deleterious both physically and spiritually, and is frequently a cause of estrangement and separation'.

In 1883 Stockham self-published a natural-childbirth book, *Tokology* (Greek for obstetrics), that was translated into French, Finnish, German and Russian – the latter had a foreword written by Leo Tolstoy. She used it to set up a sexual precursor to the *Big Issue*, giving copies to penniless women and former prostitutes to sell door-to-door. In a further entrepreneurial twist, each copy included a gift voucher for a free gynaecological exam at her clinic. The book might have been about childbirth, but it also promoted her new passion – karezza. Others latched on to the idea at the same time: A.E. Newton wrote *The Better Way*; and Paschal Beverly Randolph published *Eulis! ... or the Anseiratic mysteries*. Stockham herself published George N. Miller's novel *Strike of a Sex*, in which he described the fictional but karezza-like 'Zugassent's Discovery'.

The karezza method is remarkably similar to the secrets found in ancient Oriental sex guides: first you prepare by reading and meditating on the divine power. Then, you start having slow, orgasmless sex. Before (or during) 'complete, quiet union of the sexual organs', couples should dedicate themselves, with the words: 'We are living spiritual beings; our bodies symbolize soul union, and in closest contact each receives strength to be more to the other and more to all the world.' Don't you love it when your partner talks holy in bed?

The ultimate goal was soul union: 'During a lengthy period of perfect control, the whole being of each is merged into the other, and an exquisite exaltation experienced,' promised Stockham. 'This may be accompanied by a quiet motion, entirely under subordination of the will, so that the thrill of passion for either may not go beyond a pleasurable exchange ... In the course of an hour the physical tension subsides, the spiritual exaltation increases, and not uncommonly visions of a transcendent life are seen and consciousness of new powers experienced.' It should, she added, be performed fortnightly, or monthly, or even less frequently, 'Scores of married men and women attest that such self-control is perfectly and easily possible.'

Not everyone was convinced. One contemporary reviewer, a Dr Sperry, wrote: 'Perhaps a few old and sexually decayed men and women can employ it quite satisfactorily. I am forced to the conclusion that average men and women, who possess fullness of sexual vigour, alert minds and live nerves, cannot indulge in sexual connection and experience a satisfactory play of the affections without passing on to coition, sexual spasm and discharge of semen. When starving men learn to hold pleasant and nutritious food in their mouths for an hour without swallowing it, then we may expect passionate men and women to adopt karezza as a practical method of healthfully enjoying the mental and physical pleasures of sexual embrace.'

Nor did karezza provoke unbridled joy among those in authority. It was effectively illegal, because at the time promoting contraception was against the law. And while the Vatican allows the rhythm method, non-orgasmic sex was beyond the pale. Forty years after Stockham's death in 1912, the papacy issued a 'solemn warning' forbidding priests and spiritual directors ever to recommend the idea. It is not, apparently, part of 'Christ's Law'.

Ida Craddock: Hounded to Death

Ida Craddock is hardly a name to conjure visions of long nights of exotic sex and supernatural couplings with heavenly paramours. Nor does she sound the sort of Victorian woman whose writings on love would either inspire generations of Satan-worshippers or get her jailed and ultimately persecuted to her death by a notoriously vindictive censor. But that indeed is our Ms Craddock.

Her life started in a puritanical enough fashion. She was born in Philadelphia in 1857 to a mother who had been interested in spiritualism but became a fundamentalist Christian after her husband died, leaving her with two-year-old Ida. The girl was brought up in a strict disciplinarian regime and learnt to read the Bible at a very early age. The result, naturally, was that in her adult years she turned to a life of occultism and promiscuous sex. At the age of 32, and a rather lumpen-looking 32 at that, she was juggling two male lovers. The first was younger, but sexually callow, the second older but reportedly an expert in Alice Stockham's tantric-sex karezza technique. This sent Craddock into unheralded ecstasies and struck her as a divine revelation. The fact that Mr Red-Hot Lover was also an ex-clergyman and a mystic helped to set her future direction. She had already joined the Unitarian faith and encountered the world of strange ideas by attending lectures by the Theosophists, who believed in astral projection, among other esoteric weirdnesses.

Craddock became a priestess and pastor of the Church of Yoga and a student of religious eroticism.

She travelled America lecturing on topics such as 'What Christianity has done for the marital relation' and offered sex counselling from a small office in Chicago. Those too shy to attend in person could send off for her mail-order sex guides – pamphlets such as *The Wedding Night* and *Right Marital Living*. These emphasized sexual self-control and warned that forcing intercourse on one's wife was effectively rape. Orders poured in from wives, progressive couples and family doctors. Today it sounds pretty straight and staid. But it clashed head-long with the convention that husbands should enjoy complete sexual power over their wives. Any open discussion of sex by a woman was bound to provoke the legion of moralists who believed such talk served only to feed monstrous vices that were eating at the heart of American society.

Several critics questioned how Ida had acquired all this sexual wisdom when she was unmarried and thus, if respectable, a virgin. Her 1894 tract *Heavenly Bridegrooms* provided a straightforward explanation. She claimed that she was in fact wedded to an angel called Soph who visited at night, when he would make love to her in all the ways a demi-god should. He also taught her a system of divine and rather difficult sexual acts, most of which involve non-ejaculatory intercourse that would bring esoteric enlightenment to whoever practised them. She explained it all in a later pamphlet, called *Psychic Wedlock*.

Craddock's inevitable clash with the authorities started in 1893, when she publicly defended a belly-dance act at the World's Columbian Exposition in Chicago against calls from Anthony Comstock, America's self-appointed arch-censor, for it to be banned. Comstock was a religious fanatic who worked for the U.S. Post Office and 20 years previously had persuaded Congress to pass the Comstock Act, which made it illegal to send 'obscene material' such as sex advice through the mail. At the end of his career, Comstock claimed to have 'convicted persons enough to fill a passenger train of 61 coaches, 60 containing sixty passengers each, and the 61st almost full'. Craddock wrote an article in the journal *The World* about how the belly dancers' undulations were an expression of sexual self-control and should be taught to married women to enhance their sex lives. Comstock declared the article obscene and banned it from being sent through the post.

Craddock had other enemies who, with the help of her mother, had her admitted to the Pennsylvania Hospital for the Insane in 1898. She was released after three months without ever being judged legally insane by a court. She did not help her case by forcing a showdown with Comstock. In 1899, she was charged with sending *Right Marital Living* through the mail and only stayed out of prison because the famed lawyer and free-speech advocate Clarence Darrow paid her bail. Then she headed for York City, Comstock's base, where she carried on her sex advice and pamphleteering. 'I have an inward feeling that I am really divinely led here to face this wicked and depraved man Comstock in open court,' she wrote.

She got her wish. In 1902, Craddock was arrested under New York's local anti-obscenity law for posting out copies of *The Wedding Night*. The judge refused to allow the jury to see the 'indescribably obscene' document. The jury found Craddock guilty and she was sentenced to three months in the harsh city workhouse. On her release, she was immediately re-arrested under another piece of Comstock legislation, the national anti-obscenity law. On the morning she was to be sentenced again, she killed herself by slashing her wrists and inhaling natural gas. In her suicide note, she launched a final counter-attack, writing, 'Perhaps it may be that in my death, more than in my life, the American people may be shocked into investigating the dreadful state of affairs which permits that unctuous sexual hypocrite Anthony Comstock to wax fat and arrogant and to trample upon the liberties of the people.' Ultimately, hers was the final victory: the negative publicity generated by Comstock's merciless hounding turned public opinion against him. Contributions to his Society for the Suppression of Vice fell sharply and his influence began to ebb.

Craddock's life and work lie buried somewhere amid history's dust heap of eccentric ideas. But her writing lives on in one odd realm. When Aleister Crowley, the devil worshipper and self-styled 'world's wickedest man', visited America ten years after Craddock's death, he read and admired her

Psychic Wedlock enough to recommend it to followers. Her ideas steadily became adopted and adapted
by satanic writers, and still turn up in books of 'Sex
Magick' spells today. Somehow, practising the dark
arts through exotic intercourse doesn't seem the
same when you know that a woman called Ida
Craddock is behind much of it.

Paschal Beverly Randolph: Sex Magician

Craddock was not the only sex advisor to influence
Crowley's sex magicians. Another was the enigmatic
figure of Paschal Beverly Randolph, an African-
American who was born in Virginia in 1825, qualified as a medical doctor and became a well-known
spiritualist who travelled through Turkey, Egypt and
Syria in search of esoteric wisdom. Crowley seems
to have derived his catchphrase 'Love is the Law,
Love under Will' from him.

The best known of Randolph's three sex-magic
manuals was the 1874 title *Eulis! The history of love:
its wondrous magic, chemistry, rules, laws, modes,
moods and rationale; being the third revelation of
soul and sex*. At the centre of Randolph's theories
were the sex rituals of the Syrian Nusairi tribe,
which he transformed into his 'Anseiratic
Mysteries'. These required a man and woman to
practise 49 days' worth of tantra-style sexual meditation, at the end of which they would orgasm so
powerfully that bursts of electro-magnetic energy
would shoot between them at seven points on their

bodies. This energy burst would put them in tele-pathic touch with divine beings from other dimen-sions and thus give them the power to become very rich by predicting the outcomes of future business deals. Or at least, that was the theory. It also prom-ised that they would be able to control other people's actions and read minds, as well as stop spouses' adultery by rendering them 'sexively cold' to others. Nice.

Despite all these powers, and although his life-long motto was 'Try!', sex-magic did not always work for Randolph. In 1875 he succumbed to chronic depression and ended his life by suicide at the age of 50, leaving a wife and infant son.

Neat Tricks

The lower-constrictor

Ananga Ranga (15th century),
translated by Sir Richard F. Burton (1885)

She must ever strive to close and constrict the yoni
until it holds the penis, as with a finger, opening and
shutting at her pleasure and finally acting as the
hand of the Gopala-girl who milks the cow. This can
only be learnt by long practice. Her husband will
then value her above all women, nor would he
exchange her for the most beautiful queen in the
three worlds. So lovely and pleasant to the man is
she-who-constricts.

The ice-pack

John Eichenlaub, *The Marriage Art* (1962)

Freezing cold against your skin stimulates both pain
and temperature nerves, which are exactly the types
of fibres that trigger sexual climax. Before intercourse, the wife places at the bedside a bowl of
crushed ice or a handful of cracked iced wrapped in a
wet towel. Both partners strip and enjoy sex, with
the husband on top.

As the husband starts his final surge to climax, the
wife picks up a handful of crushed ice or the cold
towel. Just as the paroxysms of orgasm start, she
jams the ice-cold poultice against her husband's
crotch and keeps it there throughout his conclusion.

The 'senior silicone'

Rennie MacAndrew, *Life Long Love:
healthy sex and marriage* (1928)

A woman with badly drooping breasts might desire to wear her brassiere. These may now be had in attractive flesh pink colour with an opening through which a small portion of breast can protrude. On the other hand, a good tip for the wife with fallen breasts is what might be called the Right Arm Trick. The arm is brought up under the bosom so as to raise it and make it firm. This makes the husband feel he is in the arms of a young girl with firm breasts, thus taking him back in memory to the happy early-married days.

The toe job

Dr Alex Comfort, *The Joy of Sex* (1972)

The pad of the big toe applied to the clitoris or the vulva is a magnificent erotic instrument ... Use the toe in mammary or armpit intercourse or anytime you are astride her, or sit facing as she lies or sits. Make sure the nail isn't sharp.

In a restaurant one can surreptitiously remove a shoe and sock, reach over, and keep her in almost continuous orgasm with all four hands fully in view on the table top and no sign of contact – a party trick which rates as really advanced sex ... She has less scope, but can learn to masturbate him with her two big toes.

Thrust your way to immortality

Mawangdui medical manuscripts (200–300 BC)

The ideal 100 thrusts

At the tenth thrust without coming, eyes and
ears are perceptive and bright

At the twentieth, the voice has beauty and
clarity

At the thirtieth, the skin glows

At the fortieth, spine and upper side become
strong

At the fiftieth, your buttocks become muscular

At the sixtieth, your life force passes freely
through you

At the seventieth, your entire life is without
calamity

At the eightieth, you have a long life

At the ninetieth, you achieve spiritual
enlightenment

At the hundredth your body enters the realm
of immortality

How to thrust - the 'ten refinements'

Mawangdui medical manuscripts (200–300 BC)

1 Go up
2 Go down
3 Go to the left
4 Go to the right
5 Thrust rapidly
6 Thrust slowly
7 Thrust rarely
8 Thrust frequently
9 Enter shallowly
10 Enter deeply

Fetishes: what's normal (and what's not)?

Havelock Ellis, *Psychology of Sex:
a manual for students* (1933)

Normal:

Hands, feet, breasts, buttocks, hair, secretions
    and excretions, odours.
Gloves, shoes, stockings and garters, aprons,
    handkerchiefs, underlinen. Statues.

Abnormal:

Lameness, squinting, smallpox scars, children,
elderly people, corpses and excitement caused
by animals. Whipping, cruelty, exhibitionism,
mutilation and murder. Watching people climb,
swing, urinate or defecate.

Weird wet dreams

Artemidoros of Daldis,
The Classification of Dreams (Greece, AD 2)

Normal:

Intercourse of a man with his wife or mistress;
with prostitutes; with a woman whom the male
dreamer does not know; with his male or
female slave; with a woman known to him and
well-acquainted with him. Intercourse between
a richer man and a poorer man, or an older man
and a younger man. A female dreamer having
sex with a man she knows.

Abnormal:

Incest. Sexual relations between male friends.

Unnatural:

Masturbation, kissing one's own penis,
practising fellatio on oneself, a woman having
sex with another woman, sexual intercourse
with a female or male deity, intercourse with
corpses or animals.

Fifteen

EDWARDIAN ENJOYMENT

Towards the end of the Victorian era, the authorities' killjoy sexual grip began finally to weaken and a new idea began to gain public acceptance: enjoyment was not only for the wicked and the weird.

In marital advice books around 1900, sexual pleasure started to become actively promoted rather than merely permitted. The march of 'social progress', of women's rights agitation and growing medical knowledge of sexual mechanics seem all to have played a part in fostering awareness of female sexual desires in the Western world. The long era of 'Brace thyself, wife' was finally ending, too: after 1910, the idea of foreplay makes a widespread comeback, having been largely absent for centuries. Women suddenly became creatures who could be turned on – but only by their husbands, and only if those husbands had learnt the secret skills.

Keep those revolutionary banners furled, though. It was hardly a free-for-all. The Viennese psychiatrist Richard Krafft-Ebing's scientific work on sexual aberration, *Psychopathia Sexualis*, was published in

1886 but not allowed into Britain until it had reached its tenth edition in 1899. Even then, the publishers would only sell it to doctors and lawyers, and some of it – the sex stuff, predictably – was printed in Latin, so that less-educated people would not understand terms such as *libido sexualis* and *frigidas uxoris*. Krafft-Ebing detailed real-life eccentricities in hundreds of case histories – the engineer who got turned on by slaughter-houses, the cobbler who stole women's clothes, the woman who thought she was a man, the merchant obsessed with self-abuse. The author was hardly a proud advocate of fetishism, though, and even attempted to cure homosexuality using hypnosis. This did not stop the *British Medical Journal* getting so angered by all the book's 'nauseous detail' that it suggested it should be 'put to the most ignominious use to which paper could be applied'. How uncomfortable.

But where mainstream, traditional, monogamous hubby'n'wifey were concerned, the whole subject of sex was becoming increasingly important – to the point where it was even acknowledged as crucial to their relationship. William J. Fielding wrote in *Sanity in Sex* in 1920 that marriage 'is fundamentally a sexual union and its success or failure, all things considered, is largely determined by considerations arising from the actual problems of sex'. The same year, Salomon Herbert warned in *Fundamentals in Sexual Ethics* that 'Woman's innate coyness keeps her from giving way to her natural impulses which often need the active stimulation of a lover before they are brought into conscious evidence.'

But how do you do that? The majority of books remained coy about the actual physical procedures which husbands needed to learn to pleasure their women. The manuals were like car-repair guides that daren't publish pictures of open bonnets or, God forbid, a lubrication system, for fear of causing shock or inviting prosecution. Many a young man would have been left scratching his head – seldom a satisfactory method of foreplay.

Physical Difficulties

Too big? Get a long wife

Giovanni Marinello, *Medicine Pertinent
to the Infirmities of Women* (Italy, 1563)

Long penises mean the sperm will get too cold
before it enters the woman. The answer? Pick a tall
bride, so her long uterus will keep the sperm warm
on its journey.

Proceed, but with caution

Theodoor Hendrik Van de Velde, *Ideal Marriage,
Its Physiology and Technique* (1928)

On the whole, a phallus of unusually large size must
be more agreeable to women on account of increased
pressure and friction in coitus. But men who know
themselves to be unusually well endowed by nature
should exercise particular care till they are quite
sure that they cause no harm to their wives.

Problem? Wot problem?

John Marten, *Gonosologium Novum,
or a new system of all secret infirmities and diseases, natural,
accidental, and venereal in men and women* (1709)

As for the bigness of a man's Yard, it very rarely
happens that any woman complains of it, or is in any
ways incommodated by it.

Oh dear!

Nicholas Venette, *The Mysteries of Conjugal Love Reveald* (1703)

The members of generation on the man's side should not be too diminutive, in such case neither having proper force to eject the seed, or capacity to fill the pudenda in such a manner as it should be.

How you can tell

Serat Candraning Wanita (*Book of Descriptions of Women*) – traditional Javanese folklore

The shape and size of a man's penis can be deduced from his thumb.

Straighten it with ants

The Secrets of Mrs Isabella Cortese (Venice, 1561)

To repair a bent penis, you will need:

Quail testicles
Oil from the inner bark of storax and from the
    elder tree
Large-winged ants
Musk
Amber from the Orient

Mix together and apply to the bent area as needed. Consider it straightened.

The perfect percy

Perfumed Garden of Sheik Nefzaoui (16th century), translated into English by Sir Richard F. Burton

The virile member, to please women, must have at most a length of the breadth of twelve fingers, or three handbreadths, and at least six fingers, or a hand and a half breadth.

There are men with members of twelve fingers, or three hand-breadths; others of ten fingers, or two and a half hands. And others measure eight fingers, or two hands. A man whose member is of lesser dimensions cannot please women.

– and if it's too small

Rub it before copulation with tepid water, until it gets red and extended by the blood flowing into it, in consequence of the heat; then anoint it with a mixture of honey and ginger, rubbing it in sedulously. Then let him join the woman; he will procure for her such pleasure that she objects to him getting off her again.

Your fate in your pants: penis reading

Ananga Ranga of Kalyanamalla (*Stage of the Love God*), by the Indian poet Kalyan Mall (16th century)

The man whose Linga is very long will be
   wretchedly poor.
The man whose Linga is very thick will ever be
   in distress.

The man whose Linga is thin and lean will be
very lucky.
And the man whose Linga is short will be a
Rajah.

That bothersome little button

Ida Craddock, *The Wedding Night* (1900)

A woman's clitoris is sometimes hooded, which, of course, is an unnatural condition, and is apt to result in sexual coldness on her part, or, at best, in a stunted sex desire. Here a physician should be appealed to, as the clitoris can be freed from its hood by circumcision; and the earlier that this is done in a girl's life the better for her health. Many a girl infant, it is now maintained by some physicians, is nervously deranged by the existence of such a hood, and would be restored to health by its circumcision.

Some women have an abnormally long clitoris, which it is impossible not to engage during coition, and such women are usually sensual, and lacking in the ability to prolong the act. In extreme cases the excision of such a clitoris may be beneficial; but it would seem preferable to first employ the milder method of suggestive therapeutics, and for the wife to endeavor to turn her thoughts from the sensation induced at the clitoris to that induced within the vagina, which is the natural and wholesome sensation to be aroused in a woman.

... It's somewhere down there

Encyclopaedia of Sex and Love Technique (1941)

Many men are not able to find this tiny organ.

But probably best ignored

Edward Podolsky, *Sex Technique for Husband and Wife* (1947)

The clitoris, while important, is not nearly as important as many of us have been taught or led to believe.

Sixteen

THE WORLD'S DULLEST SEX BOOK

If Otto Weininger achieved nothing else, he can justifiably claim to be among the earliest pioneers of the James Dean/Marilyn Monroe/Sid Vicious effect – i.e. if you really want to sell lots of product, you've got to kill yourself first.

And how else, in Weininger's case, could you ever hope to flog huge numbers of the world's most boring book on sex?

Written at the dawn of the twentieth century, *Sex and Character* managed to avoid anything erotic, exotic or even particularly interesting in favour of a morass of neo-Freudianism, middle-European angst, anti-Semitism and obscure metaphysics inspired largely by the philosophers Kant and Nietzsche, neither of whom is known for their comic repertoire. Weininger's tract on sexuality was only good for the bedside table if you suffered from insomnia or premature ejaculation. He started with the premise that individual men and women exist at various points on a spectrum that runs from masculinity to femininity – and in the middle there is no real difference at all. He then proceeded to create mathematical and logical formulae to explain the rules of sexual attraction, namely: 'For sexual union always a complete man (M) and a complete woman (W) strive to come together, even if, in every given case, [sexual identity] is distributed upon the two different individuals in varied proportion.' Indeed.

Then there are also, apparently, things called detumescence and contrection drives and, 'While M in fact possesses both, detumescence and contrection drive, in W a genuine detumescence drive is not present at all. This is already given by the fact that, in the sexual act, W does not deposit something to M, but only M to W: W retains the male as well as the female secretions.' And so it goes on, with few opportunities for light relief, bar the odd strange assertion such as, 'Woman is nothing but sexuality, she is sexuality itself, and falls into two classes: the maternal type and the prostitute.'

Weininger, an Austrian Jew who converted to Christianity, wrote the book at a tender 21. He was convinced that his genius was just waiting to be discovered. Soon after the book's publication he went to Italy to await news of its inevitable blockbuster success. But neither the sales nor the resulting adulation seemed forthcoming. Over the ensuing months he went into a deep mental decline, described by friends as 'a too grave sense of responsibility'. On 4 October 1903, aged 23, he shot himself in the house in Vienna where Beethoven, the man Weininger considered one of the world's greatest geniuses, had died.

In publicity terms, at least, it proved a shrewd move. News of the tragic young writer's death quickly spread and Weininger became a cause célèbre, inspiring several imitation suicides. *Sex and Character* began to sell. August Strindberg gave it an effusive review, saying it 'probably solved the hardest of all problems' – the 'woman problem'. Unlikely, but nevertheless the book ran through printing after printing. It was translated into numerous languages, and in a few years his publishers declared that no scientific book in the history of publishing had achieved greater success. If heaven has a corner reserved for posthumous achievers, Weininger will be there now, swapping hard-luck stories with Van Gogh and Buddy Holly.

Crisis Talks

How to recognize a female orgasm

Mawangdui medical manuscripts (200–300 BC)

The nose sweats and the lips are white: the hands and feet all twitch; the buttocks do not adhere to the bed mat, but rise up and away. When she becomes relaxed there her sexual essence spreads out. At this point the chi expands in the uterus. Essence and spirit enter and are deposited, then spiritual enlightenment takes place.

Girls: how to fake it

Ovid's poem, *Ars Amatoria*
(*The Art of Love*) (c. I BC)

Feel the pleasure in the very marrow of your bones; share it fairly with your lover, say pleasant, naughty things the while. But if Nature has withheld from you the sensation of pleasure, then teach your lips to lie and say you feel it all.

Unhappy is the woman who feels no answering thrill. But, if you have to pretend, don't betray yourself by over-acting. Let your movements and your eyes combine to deceive us, and, gasping, panting, complete the illusion.

Men: how to stop it

Fang-nei-pu-I (Healthy Sex Life), by the Taoist physician Sun Szu-mo
(AD 601–682)

Every time a man feels he is about to emit semen during the sexual act, he should close his mouth and open his eyes wide, hold his breath and firmly control himself. He should move his hands up and down and hold his breath in his nose, constraining the lower part of his body so that he breathes with his abdomen.

Straightening his spine, he should quickly press the P'ing-I Point [a point at the perineum, twixt scrotum and anus] with the index and middle finger of his left hand, then let out his breath, at the same time gnashing his teeth a thousand times. In this manner the semen will ascend and benefit the brain, thus lengthening one's span of life.

Delay it with monkeys

Koka Shastra (The Scripture of Koka),
by the Indian poet Kokkoka (12th century)

Direct your thoughts to rivers, woods, caves, mountains or other pleasant places, and imagine proceeding through them gently and slowly. If you imagine a particularly nimble monkey swinging on the branch of a tree, you will not ejaculate even though your semen is already at the tip of your penis.

An old boy-scout trick

Giovanni Marinello, *Medicine Pertinent to the Infirmities of Women* (Italy, 1563)

If the man orgasms before the woman does, she cannot get pregnant. So tie string around the husband's testicles so sperm cannot escape. When the wife feels ready to orgasm, she can untie the knot.

Or consider cannabis

Castore Durante, *New Herbarium* (Rome, 1585)

How to delay climax: try cannabis ... Or if you can't get that, wild mint?

Seventeen

ELLIS, THE IMPOTENT ICON

One of Britain's most eminent marital writers never got far beyond foreplay – and strange games of foreplay at that.

It's a hotly fought contest, but Havelock Ellis has a strong case for being the most messed up sex advisor ever published.

Ellis, a doctor, was born near London in 1859 and made a career as an author, with sex his main subject. Why? In his book, *Sex and Marriage*, he claims he dedicated his professional life to fighting the institutional ignorance and denial he grew up with. On the other hand, the most obvious explanation is also the most probable – he was trying to compensate for his deep sexual inadequacies. His series of books, called *Studies in the Psychology of Sex*, ran to seven volumes and was published between 1897 and 1928 – but only the first, about homosexuality, titled *Sexual Inversion* (which claimed that being gay was genetic), was published in Britain in his lifetime. It was promptly banned. The bookseller responsible pleaded guilty to a charge of obscene publication in 1898 and the judge

called the text a 'pretence and a sham'. Ellis had to
publish the rest of the series in America.

Physically, Ellis stood tall, solemn and gentle,
with a high, squeaky voice. His ideas were heavily
influenced by James Hinton, who founded the first
Victorian sex cult and argued that women should get
fun from sex. And while Ellis scandalized late-
Victorian England by suggesting that sexual expression was a normal, healthy human function, many
would argue that his own sex life was quite the
opposite. He was attracted to women, but for most of
his life could only manage solo and mutual masturbation. His biggest thrill was to watch his lover
urinate, a function that he considered mystical in its
beauty. As for heterosexual intercourse, Ellis's fears
are exposed in his 1933 book, *Psychology of
Marriage*, in which he warns young men that, after
their first bout of sex, they are in danger of fainting,
vomiting, involuntary urination, defecation, epileptic fits and 'lesions of various organs, even rupture
of the spleen'. Older men, he says, are in peril of
dropping dead.

Where his own sexuality led, his work followed,
charting the strange, the odd and the distasteful –
things no decent Victorian or Edwardian publicly
acknowledged. It is all standard fare for today's
fetish mags and websites, but Ellis's subjects' stories
came as a Richter-sized shock. One example was a
government official whose obsession with squeaky
footwear was sparked by his first sexual experience,
on a staircase with a woman who had a creaking
shoe. There was also a lecturer who derived sexual

pleasure from burning his skin with hot wires. Part of the shock was caused by the fact that his deviants were frequently middle-class professionals. But then Ellis thought society was rather messed up. He wrote that the high rate of suicide in civilization 'means that the population is winding up its nervous and intellectual system to the utmost point of tension and that sometimes it snaps'.

His solution sounds straight out of a modern pop-psychology book: just accept that whatever floats your boat is cool: 'It is important always to bear in mind that whatever gives satisfaction and relief to both parties is good and right, and even in the best sense normal, provided – as is not likely to happen in sound and healthy persons – no injury is effected,' he wrote. Shame it didn't work for Ellis. His long romantic and intellectual connection with the South African novelist Olive Schreiner started when he wrote her fan mail. They first met after a long exchange of letters. He was swept away. Schreiner wept with disappointment. She found him insufficiently virile. In fact, he proved physically unable to consummate the relationship. He had the same trouble with other women. Schreiner, on the other hand, suffered at the hands of a powerful libido: she used to take large doses of potassium bromide to try to reduce her sex drive. Ellis subsequently married Edith Lees, in 1891. She was an English writer with strong lesbian preferences who apparently resembled Dylan Thomas. He was still a virgin, and at the end of the honeymoon returned to his bachelor rooms in Paddington. They hoped to find companionship and freedom in a 'rational' union (as if such things exist) and Ellis seemed happy to let her find satisfaction outside marriage. He chose homosexuality for his first book partly because of his curiosity about his wife's lesbianism. She was his case history number 38.

Despite his impotence, Ellis was a magnet for highly sexed women. American ladies sent him intimate letters about their sex problems, along with nude photographs of themselves. Many visited him and were smitten, only to be disappointed by their sex guru's physical incapacity. But when Ellis fell in love with the American birth-control campaigner Margaret Sanger (see page 217), Edith attempted suicide several times and declined into madness and death. Ellis was distraught, but carried on his affair anyway. He died in 1939, which might be considered fortunate as he had become enthralled by the idea of Nazi eugenic breeding programmes that could wipe out the 'unfit' and create a genetically elite technocracy who would apply scientific panaceas to Britain's social sickness. The outcome of the Second World War might well have proved a disappointment to him.

Vintage Viagra

First, extract the king's teeth ...

Ratimanjari of Jayadeva (The Posy of Love)
(India, *c.* 16th century)

A woman wets immediately if she is sprinkled with powder made from two teeth of a king, mixed with the two wings of a bee, powdered, and a petal blown by the wind from a funeral wreath.

Drink wasps

Mawangdui medical manuscripts (200–300 BC)

Collect swarming beetle larvae in the fifth month on the full-moon day. Put them in a bamboo tube. Set it in a slotted steaming pot and cook. You may need to take this medicine several times.

Or –
Take 20 wasp larvae and place them in one cup of sweet liquor and drink it at midday. The tonic is good for ten bouts of sex.

Or –
Dry in the dark snails removed from the shell and crush them. If you want 20 bouts of sex, use seven pinches; if you want ten, use three pinches – and one cup of liquor.

Perk it up with pistachios

Dr Leonardo Fioravanti, *La Cirugia* (Venice, 1570)

You will need:

20 chestnuts
4oz pistachios
ragwort
cinnamon
cubebs
sugar

Take the lot and boil it all down to an elixir. Then drink. Sorted.

Parsnips or bruised acorns?

Aristotle's Works, Containing the Masterpiece. Directions for midwives, counsel and advice to childbearing women, with various useful remedies (London, c. 1860)

Erection is chiefly caused by eringoes [the candied roots of sea-holly], cresses, parsnips, artichokes, turnips, asparagus, candied ginger, acorns bruised to powder and drank in muscadel, scallion [green onions], sea shellfish, etc.

Camel fat

Perfumed Garden of Sheik Nefzaoui (16th century),
translated into English by Sir Richard F. Burton

A man who would wish to acquire vigour for coition
may melt down fat from the hump of a camel, and
rub his member with it just before the act; it will
then perform wonders, and the woman will praise it
for its work

– or overdose on eggs

A man who wishes to copulate during a whole night,
and whose desire, having come on suddenly, will not
allow him to prepare himself and follow the regimen
just mentioned, may have recourse to the following
recipe. He must get a great number of eggs, so that
he may eat to surfeit, and fry them with fresh fat
and butter; when done he immerses them in honey,
working the whole mass well together. He must then
eat of them as much as possible with a little bread,
and he may be certain that for the whole night his
member will not give him any rest.

Try potatoes

Nicholas Venette, *The Mysteries of Conjugal Love Reveal'd* (1703)

There are certain meats by which the seed is increased, as radishes, pullets, pigs, veal, new-laid eggs and the like. There are some meats that provoke lust, as oysters, crabs, prawns, potatoes, sweet wine, and some sorts of electuaries [medicinal pastes made from powdered herbs].

Or simply get bored

Giovanni Sinibaldi, *Rare Verities, the Cabinet of Venus Unlock'd* (1658)

The best aphrodisiacs are rest, boredom, sleep and red meat - followed by wine, prosperity, fun, music and pleasant surroundings.

Then get plastered

Smarakridalaksana (*The Art of Love Play*) (Bali, 19th century)

Obtain the penis of a wild boar, then roast it until it's done.

Eat it with galangal, garlic, seven black pepper corns, and sea salt.

Then chant this mantra:

> 'Om. I become the God of love, with a penis like
>   the penis of a boar.
> My penis is vigorous, entering the pure hole of
>   a virgin woman.
> If the boar's penis is defeated by earth, my penis
>   will be sexually defeated by her vagina in sex.
> If the boar's penis is not defeated by earth, my
>   penis will not be defeated by her vagina.
> It is untiring, it is untiring, it is untiring.'

Then, after eating the roasted boar's penis, drink aged
rice wine until you are drunk.

And chill out

Frederick Hollick, *The Male Generative Organs
in Health and Disease* (1848)

There is one drug brought from the East Indies, the
Cannabis Indica, which is the most regular in its
action and produces the most constant beneficial
effects of anything yet tried. It appears to act as a
special nervous stimulant, exciting that part of the
brain which influences the sexual organs, so that
they feel directly an increase of power ... I do not
hesitate to say that I have seen more restoration to
sexual power and more cures of sterility in both
sexes from the use of this preparation than from any
other means and I do not hesitate to pronounce it, in
certain cases, an infallible remedy.

One for the ladies ...

Giovanni Marinello, *Medicine Pertinent to the Infirmities of Women* (Italy, 1563)

Find 90 of the little grubs that live in plants that give off milk, such as the thistle. Throw them in a litre of old olive oil. Leave in the sun for seven days. Rub it on your loins and between your backside and penis.

This will give her a great experience she will really appreciate.

Eighteen

SCOUTING FOR BOYS: UNCUT

There were some who advocated manly alternatives to sex such as Britain's legendary espionage
agent, hero of the siege of Mafeking and founder
of the Boy Scout movement, Lord Baden-Powell.

He pointed out in *Rovering to Success*, a life guide
for adolescent lads published in 1922, 'Sex is not
everything in life and other energies take the place
of sex and relieve the strain. The energy that the
primitive male animal puts almost solely into sex, in
the human, is turned into all sorts of other activities
such as art, science and a hundred and one other
things. Now you can see how Rovering comes in.
Instead of aimless loafing and smutty talks you will
find lots to do in the way of hiking and enjoyment of
the out-of-door manly activities. Without knowing it
you are putting something in the place of sex.'

It certainly worked for Baden-Powell, the war
hero who wanted to be a boy for ever, and thought
that if he ever married, it would be to 'a sort of girl
Peter Pan'. In his fifties, he met Olave, who proved
to be just such a sturdy mate. He was first attracted
to his bride when he spotted her strutting manfully

down a London street. If Baden-Powell was in fact gay it remained strictly suppressed. What we can be sure of is that he could not be bothered with any of that messy sex nonsense. Perhaps Olave agreed. She seems not to have minded that her husband, having reluctantly consummated the marriage, subsequently took to sleeping out on the balcony.

But Baden-Powell's most graphic warning of the dangers of masturbation had to wait 96 years before finally landing on our bookshelves. In the original manuscript of his biggest-selling book, *Scouting for Boys*, he sought to warn his youthful troop how he had 'seen boys as young as 12 years, or slightly more, in insane asylums from excesses of this kind'. The first draft included two pages of warnings as to how the insidious evil of Onanism could cause heart problems and diseases that rotted away men's mouths, noses and eyes, ruin sex organs and lead to insanity. 'You all know what it is to have at times a pleasant feeling in your private parts, and there comes an inclination to work it up with your hand or otherwise,' suggested Baden-Powell. 'Well, lots of fellows, from not knowing any better, please themselves in this way until it often becomes a sort of habit with them which they cannot get out of. A very large number of the lunatics on our asylums have made themselves ill by indulging in this vice although at one time they were sensible cheery boys like you.'

But in 1908, his publisher, C. Arthur Pearson, and the printer thought the content obscene and a row ensued with Baden-Powell. Eventually the printer won the argument simply by stopping his presses until Baden-Powell gave way. The passages were only reinstated nearly a century later after a historian discovered the tracts and restored them to a 2004 reprint – which was sadly far too late for any aged former scouts still shakily wandering the corridors of the world's insane asylums.

How to Conceive

He shoots, he scores

Guide to Pregnancy, by Italian physician
Michele Savonarola (15th century)

In order to enter, the man must give many caresses ...
and consider the readiness of his wife; then, he must
move in and out, in this way he will succeed. Then he
must attempt to release all his sperm in one burst,
not in dribbles, nor must he raise or lower himself,
as is commonly done for pleasure, but instead
remain fixed in the hole so that the air cannot enter
and corrupt the seed.

Look out of the window, check your watch and diary

Fang Nei Chi (Records of the Bedchamber),
Sui Dynasty (AD 590–618)

A child conceived during daytime will be given
    to vomiting.
A child conceived at midnight, when the
    interaction of Heaven and Earth is at a
    standstill, will either be mute, deaf or blind.
A child conceived during a solar eclipse will
    either be burned or wounded.
A child conceived during thunder or lightning, a
    time when Heaven in its anger displays its
    might, will easily develop mental troubles.
A child conceived during a lunar eclipse will be
    persecuted by an ill fate and so will its mother.

A child conceived when there is a rainbow in
   the sky will be exposed to ill fortune.
A child conceived during the summer or winter
   solstice will bring harm to its parent.
A child conceived on nights of the waxing or
   waning moon will be killed in war or blinded
   by the wind.
A child conceived during intoxication or after a
   heavy meal will suffer from epilepsy, boils
   and ulcers.

The 16th day of the fifth moon is the day when
Heaven and Earth mate. On this day one should
refrain from sexual intercourse. Those who offend
against this taboo will die within three years.

Turn yourself over ...

Marie Stopes, *Married Love* (1918)

The position of the mouth of the womb and the relation of the vaginal canal may be such that the
spermatic fluid tends to be lost without any of it
penetrating the orifice of the womb itself. To overcome this, it is often sufficient for the woman to
turn over directly the act of union is complete and
lie face downwards for a few hours.

... and stay still

Lucretius, *On the Nature of the Universe, Book IV*

Women are thought to conceive oftener when on all fours, because the organs absorb the seed better when they are lying on their breast with loins upraised. Nor do our wives have any need of lascivious movements; for a woman can hamper conception if in her pleasure she thrusts away from the man's penis with her buttocks, making her body floppy with sinuous movements. She diverts the furrow from the straight course of the ploughshare and makes the seed fall wide of the plot. These tricks are employed by prostitutes to avoid getting laid up by pregnancy and at the same time making intercourse more attractive to men. But obviously our wives do not need any of this.

Cross your legs

Nicholas Venette, *The Mysteries of Conjugal Love Reveald* (1703)

After the act of copulation, the woman should take rest and, if it be possible, not make water for some hours. When she rises from bed, let her not do anything to disquiet herself, but walk gently up and down.

Gather yellow things and avoid dirty books

Su-nu-miao-lun (*Admirable Discourses of the Plain Girl*)
(Japan, 1592–1596), *rehashed from Chinese works* (c. 250 BC)

The Emperor asked: 'But what methods can those childless couples employ yet to obtain children?'

The Plain Girl answered, 'The way to have offspring is to bring first both yin and yang in complete harmony. One's clothes and the coverlets and pillows of the couch should all be made of yellow gauze or silk [yellow was thought to be the colour of the fertile earth]. Then on an auspicious day when according to the almanac, sun and moon are in conjunction, the man should write the day and hour on which he was born, and also those of his wife, on a tablet of pine-wood and place that on the couch.

'Moreover, on the third day of the ninth lunar month he should take a piece of wood from a peach tree [symbolic of women's genitalia and of fertility in general], the branches of which grow in an easterly direction, and thereon write his name and surname and those of his wife, then insert that piece of wood in the canopy of their couch.

'Then, on the third or fourth day after the woman's menstruation, the couple should bathe and burn incense, and pray to the spirits of heaven and earth. Only after these preparations may they ascend the couch and unite themselves. At that time the woman's womb is not yet closed and she shall conceive.

'The couple should keep their minds pure and free from all sorrow. They should not engage in accessory sexual play, not partake of aphrodisiacs and not look together at albums of erotic pictures. If they offend against these rules, both the parents and their unborn child shall be harmed.'

Hot food and drunkenness

Albertus Magnus, *De Secretis Mulierum*
(*The Secrets of Women*) (c. 1478)

Note that if the womb and intestine of a hare are dried and pulverized they become very hot, and similarly a pig's liver is hot in itself, and these will generate heat sufficient for conception. This should be eaten by her in the end of the menstrual period, because the womb is dry in this time, and somewhat hotter than usual because of the retreat of menstrual cold.

There are also other experiments. Let a woman take the herb camphor in a pulverized form and drink it with wine and she will conceive. If the urine of a man is drunk, it will impede conception. If she takes powder made from the vulva of a hare mixed with liquid honey, and adds a bull's heart, slowly bringing this to a boil, and consumes this during one week at a particular time of day, then she will conceive.

The woman ought to eat good, hot foods, and she should become a little inebriated and should be well massaged, and she should take care that her elevated legs do not cause the semen to spill out, so that she immediately exerts effort to retain it, and sleeps right afterward; in this case without doubt she will conceive.

It's all about timing

Nicholas Venette, *The Mysteries of Conjugal Love Reveald* (1703)

The eggs are best fecundated when a woman is nearest the time of her courses, by reason of the greater porosity of her womb and testicles, whereby the seminal air is the easier received into the eggs ...

The morning appears to be the more proper for generation: for after a man has agreeably diverted himself with his wife and has taken a little nap after his lawful pleasures, he soon repairs what losses he has had and quickly cures the weariness he has brought upon himself in love. Then he rises and goeth about his ordinary concerns, his wife continuing some while a-bed, to preserve the precious charge he hath entrusted her with.

Who's firing blanks? His'n'hers test

Anon., *The Treasury of Natural Secrets* (Italy, c. 16th century)

Pour barley seeds into two pots.
The man urinates in one, the woman in the other.
Then place the pots in a humid place for ten days.
The pot that fails to germinate points to the
    infertile partner.

Shoot with the right or left

Nicholas Venette, *The Mysteries of Conjugal Love Reveald* (1703)

From the right testicle cometh the male, and from the left, the female.

Goat's hair and donkey milk

Albertus Magnus, *De Secretis Mulierum* (*The Secrets of Women*) (c. 1478)

Let her place a goat's hair in the milk of a female donkey and let her tie this around her at the navel while she has sexual intercourse with her husband, and she will conceive.

Avoid indigestion

Michele Savonarola, *To Ferrara Women on Care during Pregnancy and of Newborns to Their Seventh Year* (Italy, late 1400s)

Know that your table wine and similar things that are hard to digest impede impregnation with a male child, because indigestion makes the seed cold and useless. For similar reasons, avoid tinctures, herbs, fruit, fish, crustaceans and other cold and moist foods; eating them will turn your seed female.

Gaze at brave men

Giovanni Marinello, *Medicine Pertinent
to the Infirmities of Women* (Italy, 1563)

Hang masculine paintings on the wall, so the woman's
mind is filled with thoughts of brave men, and that's
what she'll conceive.

Lie on your right side

*Aristotle's Works, Containing the Masterpiece. Directions for
midwives, counsel and advice to childbearing women, with various
useful remedies* (London, c. 1860)

In the cavity of the womb there are two cells, or
receptacles, for the seed, divided by a line running
through the midst of it. In the right side of the cavity,
by reason of the heat of the liver, males are
conceived; and in the left side, by the coldness of the
spleen, females. Most of our moderns hold this as an
infallible truth.

- and for a girl
The best time to beget a female is when the moon is
in the wane, in Libra or Aquarius.

Put your hand down there and pray

Perfumed Garden of Sheik Nefzaoui (16th century),
translated into English by Sir Richard F. Burton

If anyone placing his hand upon the vulva of a woman
that is with child pronounces the following words, 'In
the name of God! may he grant salutation and mercy
to his Prophet (salutation and mercy be with him).
Oh! my God! I pray to thee in the name of the
Prophet to let a boy issue from this conception', it
will come to pass by the will of God, and in consid-
eration for our lord Mohammed (the salutation and
grace of God be with him), the woman will be deliv-
ered of a boy.

Pregnancy tests

*Aristotle's Works, Containing the Masterpiece. Directions for
midwives, counsel and advice to childbearing women, with various
useful remedies* (London, c. 1860)

Keep the urine of the woman close in a glass for
three days and then strain it through a fine linen
cloth; if you find small living creatures in it, she hath
conceived.

Or -
Take a handsome green nettle, put it into the urine of
the woman; cover it close, and let it remain a whole
night. If the woman be with child, it will be full of
red spots on the morrow; if she is not, it will be
blackish.

Or –

At night on going to bed, let her drink water and honey, and if afterwards she feels a beating pain in her stomach and about the navel, she has conceived.

Or –

Throw a clean needle into the woman's urine, put it into a basin and let it stand all night. If it is covered with red spots in the morning, she has conceived, but if it has turned black and rusty, she has not.

Unhealthy mother? Knit with pink wool

Perfumed Garden of Sheik Nefzaoui (16th century),
translated into English by Sir Richard F. Burton

If the woman remains always in good health from the time that her pregnancy is certain, if she preserves the good looks of her face and a clear complexion, if she does not become freckled, then it may be taken as a sign that the child will be a boy.

The red colour of the nipples also points to a child of the male sex. The strong development of the breasts, and bleeding from the nose, if it comes from the right nostril, are signs of the same purport.

The signs pointing to the conception of a child of the female sex are numerous. I will name them here: frequent indisposition during pregnancy, pale complexion, spots and freckles, pains in the matrix, frequent nightmares, blackness of the nipples, a heavy feeling on the left side, nasal haemorrhage on the same side.

Boy or girl?

Aristotle's Works, Containing the Masterpiece. Directions for midwives, counsel and advice to childbearing women, with various useful remedies (London, c. 1860)

The woman breeds a boy easier and with less pain than a girl, and is more nimble. The male child is first felt by her on her right side, for male children lie on the right side of the womb. The woman, when she riseth up from a chair, doth sooner stay herself upon her right hand than her left.

The bellie lies rounder and higher than when it is a female. The right breast is harder and more plump than the left, and the right nipple redder. The colour of a woman is not so swarthy as when she conceives a girl. The contrary to these are signs of the conception of a female.

If the circle under the right eye is of a wan blue colour, be more apparent and most discoloured she is carrying a boy; if the marks be most apparent in her left eye, she carries a girl.

Let a drop of her milk fall into a basin of fair water, if it sinks to the bottom, as it drops in, round in a drop, it is a girl; but if it be a boy, it will spread and swim on the top.

Nineteen

TROUBLE DOWN UNDER

The paranoid pioneer William Chidley was a bearded, earnest-looking man who believed he could best set a living sexual example to the people of Australia if he walked around dressed in a toga.

He set out his ideas in a 1911 pamphlet entitled *The Answer*. Australians should change to a life of nudity, a diet of fruit and nuts and a 'correct' method of sexual intercourse, Chidley declared. He apparently based his theory on observations of the sex life of horses. Yet it wasn't his ideas on intercourse that got him repeatedly arrested, but his silk toga-like tunic which the authorities considered indecent. He wore it because he believed that heavy clothing caused erections. And erections would lead to sexual overexcitement, ill health and an untimely death, as well as being 'ugly things' of which 'we are all ashamed'.

Chidley's erectophobia was stark proof that Victorian guilt was alive and thriving in early 20th-century Australia. He believed his erection-free scheme would some day save the world 'from all its misery, disease, crime, and ugliness'. Conventional sexual intercourse was killing us, he warned in *The Answer*: 'Our present coitus is a perversion and a shock. Any protoplasm that receives a shock contracts, and the brain actually becomes smaller as time goes on, through the repeated shocks of coition and becomes distorted in shape. The blood supply is perverted also, and this contributes towards the injury.' To assist his case, the pamphlet contained line drawings showing married couples steadily deteriorating under the continual strain of lovemaking: 'The delicate network of muscles on face and the eyes show it more plainly than any other part of the body.'

Chidley had been born in 1860 in Victoria and was adopted as an infant by a toyshop owner who, it seems, belonged to an early free-love sect. But that did not stop the adolescent Chidley suffering torments of guilt and fear over his frequent masturbation: he had read a pamphlet by 'a medical man in Melbourne' which warned how his habit would lead to insanity and dissolution. Indeed, he grew up to become a photographer, painter and illustrator, living a rock'n'roll life of sex and drink. In 1882 he was in court on manslaughter charges following a street brawl. He was acquitted and soon afterwards met an actress, Ada Grantley, with whom he sporadically lived and travelled until she died in 1908.

Her death hit him hard and Chidley became convinced that she had been killed by sexual overindulgence, a belief he felt was supported by contemporary advice books, which warned against excessive intercourse. When, as a teenager, he had visited the public library to learn about sex, a manual had warned him, 'There is little or no difference between the results of excessive coition and those of self-abuse.' At the age of 50, he decided to go public with his theory of healthy sexual technique and in 1911 took his pamphlet on to the streets of Melbourne, explaining 'natural coition' to anyone prepared to be ranted at by a sex freak dressed as an Ancient Greek. To avoid the debilitating effects of erections, his system involved maintaining a flaccid penis that was sucked by vacuum force into the vagina. Weird, yes, but a logically distorted result of all the sexual-restraint propaganda flying about.

The authorities did not see it that way. Trying to sell these ideas on the streets of Sydney between 1912 and 1915 got him jailed repeatedly for indecency. Eventually he was confined in a mental hospital. His sanity was even debated in the New South Wales Parliament, not least because Chidley had managed to line up a series of eminent mainstream medics who agreed in court that intercourse could damage the nervous system because orgasm caused a 'brainstorm' and 'nervous shocks in high degree', and that 'nerve disturbance consequent upon coitus might lead to heart trouble'.

He was not without support from high society either. Australian intellectuals formed a Chidley defence committee to spring him from incarceration. He also exchanged letters and ideas with the English sexologists Edward Carpenter and Havelock

Ellis. Chidley sent Ellis an account of his sexual experiences, which the latter used in one of his studies. His greatest influence in the end, however, was in helping to create a backlash against censorship. Popular support for Chidley's right to speak about sex grew, to the point where it embarrassed the state government. After Chidley died in 1916, his strange beliefs lived on for a while with a small band of followers continuing his oddball campaign through the 1920s.

Inconceivable Ideas

Sob-stoppers

Giovanni Sinibaldi, *Rare Verities,
the Cabinet of Venus Unlock'd* (1658)

A sad or weeping woman cannot conceive.

Coitus inter-ructions

*Onania, or the heinous sin of self-pollution, and all its frightful
consequences, in both sexes, considered: with spiritual and physical
advice to those who have already injured themselves by this
abominable practice* (1712)

When the man, by a criminal untimely retreat, disappoints his wife's as well as his own fertility, this is what truly may be call'd a frustraneous abuse of their bodies, and must be an abominable sin. Yet it is certain, that thousands there are in the married state, who provoke and gratify their lust, as far as is consistent with this their destructive purpose, and no farther.

Crime against wife

Theodoor Hendrik Van de Velde, *Ideal Marriage,
Its Physiology and Technique* (1928)

For sexually adequate, sensitive and vitally vigorous people, systematic coitus interruptus means not only a degradation but also an extermination of the marital relationship: a danger to the husband's health and a crime against the wife.

Suspended stimulation

Marie Stopes, *Married Love* (1918)

Coitus interruptus, while it may have saved the woman the anguish of bearing unwanted children, is yet very harmful to her, and is to be deprecated. It tends to leave the woman in mid-air, as it were; to leave her stimulated and unsatisfied and therefore it has a very bad effect on her nerves and general health, particularly if it is done frequently.

The woman, too, loses the advantage of the partial absorption off the man's secretions. It is extremely likely that the highly stimulating secretions which accompany man's semen can and do penetrate and affect the woman's whole organism.

Twenty

CULT OF THE VIRGIN MARIE

Marie Carmichael Stopes is further proof, if any more were needed, that you don't need relevant experience to become a leading world expert on lovemaking.

Quite the opposite. Although she was married and in her late 30s when she wrote one of Britain's best-selling and most enduring sex guides, *Married Love*, she was also still a virgin.

Stopes was exceptionally bright – and a frighteningly difficult egotist. Born into a middle-class family in Edinburgh in 1880, she was the first woman to join Manchester University's science department as a lecturer. She also gained three degrees in botany and obtained a doctorate, becoming Britain's youngest doctor of science. She was also an authority on the composition of coal. But she was neither lucky in love nor in bed. During a sabbatical from Manchester University to perform geological research, she had gone in pursuit of a Japanese professor who responded to her advances by running home to Japan. Soon after, she married a gentle Canadian called Reginald 'Ruggles' Gates who, sadly for him, is best remembered for failing ever to get 'effectively' rigid. It was a while before Stopes thought there was anything wrong with her marriage, but eventually she got worried that she had not become pregnant and went rummaging in the British Museum's private cupboard, to which she had access as a scientist. This led her to conclude that her marriage had never been consummated.

'I had never been fully penetrated by a normal male organ,' she recalled five years later in the divorce court. 'I only remember three occasions on which it was partially rigid, and then it never got effectively rigid.' Perhaps, though, Gates was simply too terrified. But Stopes had some idea of what she was missing; she had subsequently read all there was to read on sex education, particularly the books of Havelock Ellis, whose work she ungratefully described later as 'like breathing soot'.

Married Love was dedicated 'to young husbands and all those who are betrothed in love' – and to that vast majority of people who are 'nearly normal'. She turned the Gates experience to her advantage, as a special plea for publishing the book, writing: 'In my first marriage, I paid such a terrible price for sex-ignorance that I feel that knowledge gained at such a cost should be placed at the service of humanity.' Stopes proved she had some political smarts, too, by claiming heavenly authorization to cover this salacious subject. She later claimed that her mission had come as a holy revelation one day when she was walking naked in the yew woods behind her home.

While publishing *Married Love*, Stopes went through the process of divorce and also became engaged to her second husband. Nevertheless, she wrote that remarriage was not a good idea: 'Many think that merely by loosening the bonds and making it possible to start afresh with someone else, their lives would be made harmonious and happy. But often such reformers forget that he or she who knows nothing of the way to make marriage great and beautiful with one partner, is not likely to succeed with another.' Perhaps this is why she obliged her second husband, Humphrey Verdon Roe, to sign a contract releasing her to have sex with other men. Roe was a Manchester manufacturer who had tried, but failed, to establish a family-planning clinic for his female workforce. It was not an essentially intimate relationship. She thought married men and women should sleep in separate bedrooms.

Married Love hit the shelves early in 1918 and outsold the best-selling fiction of the era by a huge margin. It ran through five editions and 17,000 copies in the first year alone. By 1925, sales had passed the half-million mark and achieved the million in the 1950s – not counting books sold in America or the Commonwealth. It was translated into French, Dutch, Swedish, German and Danish. Stopes sent a copy to the future Queen Elizabeth on her wedding, though there is no indication that she read it. Marie's best stylistic trick was to make sex sound full of beauty and rapture, rather than guilty and mechanical. Her main innovation was to popularize the idea of a rhythmic female 'sex tide' that dictated the ebb and flow of feminine desire. In normal women, she wrote, this reached its peak once a fortnight (we can probably guess this simply reflected her own libido). And woe betide the man who got it wrong: 'A husband who desires lasting and mutual happiness in his marriage will carefully study his wife, observe how far she has a normal rhythm ... He will then endeavour to adapt his demands on her so that they are in harmony with her nature.' Failure will leave him with 'the tragic figure of the loving woman whose love tide is at the highest, and whose husband does not recognize the delicate signs of her ardour'.

Stopes had, she claimed, discovered this tide through scientific study of women whose husbands were frequently away: 'Such women, yearning daily for the tender comradeship and nearness of their husbands, find at particular times an accession of longing for the close physical union of the final sex-act. Those I have asked to keep note of the dates, have, with remarkable unanimity, told me that these times came specially just before, and some week or so after, the close of menstruation, coming, that is, about every fortnight.'

QED. Happy wives – and happy husbands too, apparently: 'Many men, who can well practise restraint for 12 to 14 days, will find that one union will then thoroughly satisfy them; and if they have the good fortune to have healthy wives, they will find that the latter too have the desire for several unions in a day or two ... Expressed in general terms, my view may be formulated thus: the mutually best regulation of intercourse in marriage is to have three or four days of repeated unions, followed by about ten days without any unions at all.'

Not only did the happy new husband have to wait ten days for sex – and any unnatural emissions in between were firmly banned – the poor chap had to ensure he didn't shoot prematurely. 'It is, perhaps, hardly an exaggeration to say that 70 or 80 per cent of our married women (in the middle classes) are deprived of the full orgasm through the excessive speed of the husband's reactions,' declared Stopes. 'So profound are woman's complex sex instincts, as well as her organs, that in rousing them the man is rousing her whole body and soul. And this takes time … as much as from ten to 20 minutes of actual physical union to consummate her feeling, while two or three minutes often completes the union for a man. The majority of wives are left wakeful and nerve-wracked.'

As for details about positions, though, readers were left to work them out for themselves – though Stopes hinted they should model themselves on sea anemonies: 'A pair should, impelled by the great wave of feeling within them, be as pliable as the sea-plants moved by the rushing tides, and they should discover for themselves which of the innumerable possible positions of equilibrium results in the greatest mutual satisfaction.'

Stopes also became Britain's leading popular authority on contraception, having published, eight months after *Married Love*, a 'practical sequel', *Wise*

Parenthood. It upset the medical profession and the Catholic Church. The technical advice covered female physiology and instructions for using the Dutch cap, and glossed over methods such as condoms, which she did not favour.

Though Stopes kept her own surname when she married, and flouted conventions of dress by going braless (and she was a well-built girl), she was hardly a model heroine for women's lib. She remained at heart a puritan reactionary, opposed to abortion and sex outside marriage. A woman's first baby should be her husband, she wrote: he needs just the simple, loving petting that is demanded by a child. She was 44 when she gave birth to her son, Harry, and became convinced he was an example of the super-race she wanted to help create through Hitlerite eugenic racial hygiene. In common with Havelock Ellis and a worryingly large proportion of her contemporaries, Stopes began to see birth control and 'proper' sexual habits as the way to realize a warped vision of a society peopled only by genetically perfect specimens, where the inferior and unworthy had been weeded out by selective breeding. She advertised through her solicitors to find a suitable child companion for young Harry and demanded that it be 'completely healthy, intelligent and uncircumcised'. She tried out four hopefuls but all were declared 'unfit to live in a decent household' with her little *übermensch*. Until he was 12 Harry was taught at home by his mother. She made him wear skirts because she feared that trousers would damage his testicles.

Harry said they became estranged when he grew up and married Mary Wallace, the daughter of the bouncing-bomb inventor, Barnes Wallace: '[Marie] said she disapproved of Mary because she was short-sighted and wore glasses, and if any of our children inherited the defect it would make a mockery of her work on eugenics.' Harry thought that, anyway, his mother simply believed that no woman could ever be worthy of him. There is another odd element in the relationship: Harry's father had co-founded the aeroplane-maker Avro, which built the Lancaster bomber that successfully dropped Mary's father's famous bombs on Germany's dams. This may not have played well with Stopes who, in 1939, had horrified her friends by sending Adolf Hitler a volume of her own poetry as a gift.

In her later years, Stopes became ever more the monstrous egotist and presumed to tell George Bernard Shaw how to write plays, and Rudyard Kipling how to compose poems. Her second marriage disintegrated; H.V. Roe was left feeling crushed and impotent. In her final years she kept a succession of young men around her, and when she died her male companion was 35 years her junior. Stopes died in 1958 a few days before her 78th birthday, still convinced almost until the end that she would live to be 120.

How to Have Strange Children

Let cats play on the lawn

Albertus Magnus, *De Secretis Mulierum*
(*The Secrets of Women*) (c. 1478)

A person who consumes sage upon which a cat has ejaculated will have kittens.

Squirt at an angle

Nicholas Venette, *The Mysteries of Conjugal Love Reveald* (1703)

If the seed be ejected lengthways into the womb, the child will be lean and tall; if otherwise, it will be thick and short.

Forget your prayers

Serat Candraning Wanita (*Book of Descriptions of Women*) –
Javanese traditional folklore

Failing to say the Islamic invocation, 'In the Name of God, the Merciful, the Compassionate', at the beginning of coitus or having intercourse in the dark will produce mentally retarded children. Talking or joking other activities during intercourse will result in a garrulous child.

Cease sex while pregnant

Marie Stopes, *Married Love* (1918)

From one distinguished medical specialist I have acquired the interesting suggestion that in one or two cases among his own patients where the prospective mother had desired unions and the husband had denied them, thinking it in her interest, the doctor had observed that the children seemed to grow up restless, uncontrollable and with an unduly marked tendency to self-abuse.

Look out, here come the DiCaprio clones

Nicholas Venette, *The Mysteries of Conjugal Love Reveald* (1703)

If the woman be young, and, in the act of copulation, be mindful of her husband, or some other friend, the child shall resemble that person then thought on: the truth of which has been proved a thousand times.

And if you do it from behind, the neighbours will know

Any children produced will be dwarfs, cripples, hunch-back'd, squinty ey'd and stupid blockheads, and by their imperfections would fully evidence the irregular life of their parents without putting us to the trouble to search the cause of such defects any further.

Twenty-one

VAN DE VELDE RECORD?

Stopes not only failed to reach her six-score years, but her best-seller was beaten on the international bookshelves by a disgraced Dutch gynaecologist. *Ideal Marriage* is perhaps the best-selling sex technique book of all time, and was first published in 1926 by Theodoor Hendrik Van de Velde.

He wrote the book in both Dutch and German and it rapidly became an international smash. In Germany alone it was reprinted 42 times, despite being placed on the *Index librorum prohibitorum,* the Catholic Church's list of banned books. Then Hitler suppressed it in 1933. By the 1970s the English translation had gone through 43 editions totalling more than a million copies. In America more than half-a-million hardcover copies were sold between 1945 and 1970.

The book sprang, once again, out of unhappiness. Van de Velde had been a successful and prosperous Dutch gynaecologist who was trapped in a stultifyingly joyless marriage when, at the age of 36, he scandalized his middle-class world by running off with a married patient, Martha Breitenstein-Hooglandt. Van de Velde had been raised by a respectable military father and had dutifully worked his way up to being appointed the director of the Haarlem Gynaecological Clinic. The adulterous affair sank him into disgrace and cost him his practice. He and Martha went into wandering exile around Europe until his wife finally granted him a divorce in 1913. The lovers married and moved to Switzerland. Whether it was as a two-fingers to his old life, or an attempt to explain the powers of sex, he began to write his blockbuster.

He was 53 when the book came out. It was dedicated to Martha but written, he said, for his patients, who were ignorant about sex. In Britain, *Ideal Marriage* caught the wave of interest in sex manuals that had been stirred by Stopes's *Married Love*. His book managed to walk a difficult legal tightrope, too. In 1930s Europe, textbooks that stressed caution and the need to keep sex within marriage would get past the authorities and be modest sellers. From there on, the more explicit they got, the more they sold – but the greater the likelihood of prosecution and pulping. In 1923, for example, copies of a pamphlet called *Family Limitations* were seized by police from a shop in Shepherds Bush, West London. The booksellers were charged with selling an obscene publication. The trouble was almost certainly caused by a drawing of the female genitalia, showing a female finger inserted to locate the cervix. The magistrate asked, 'Would you put such a book in the hands of a boy or girl of 16?'

Van de Velde was pushing his luck, and he knew it. In the book's introduction, he declared: 'I know that it will have many unpleasant results for me, for I have gradually attained to some knowledge of my fellow human beings and of their habit of condemning what is unusual and unconventional.' In the doctor's favour, though, he stressed early on that he was prescribing healthy, normal, hetero married sex and wished to 'keep the Hell-gate of the realm of sexual perversions firmly closed'. Nevertheless, he argued that oral sex was an acceptable form of foreplay – so long as it was done with caution. 'The husband must exercise the greatest gentleness, the most delicate reverence,' he warned. He added the wife should not start fellating too early in the marriage – which can hardly have played well with husbands. In addition, he suggested that unsatisfied wives should masturbate after intercourse, and recommended that sex involve love bites and 'playful' slaps.

Risqué business, but Van de Velde was at heart a Dutch conservative, declaring: 'I address myself to married men, for they are naturally educators and initiators of their wives in sexual matters.' And one of his apparent innovations, the need to spice up long marriages with variety, harks back to the earliest Indian and Arabic texts. Positions? Whatever doesn't hurt, won't hurt, he declared: 'There are numberless delicate differentiations and modifications of sexual pleasure, all lying strictly within the bounds of normality, which can banish the mechanical monotony of the too-well known from the marriage-bed and give new attractions to conjugal intercourse. What is physiologically sound may also be considered ethically sound.' He then enumerated and explained ten different positions in such a dull and pedantic manner that they would struggle to reach the same erotic plane as the assembly leaflet for an Ikea coffee table.

Afterplay was Van de Velde's other great rediscovery. 'It is an essential and most significant act in the love drama, but unfortunately the most neglected of all,' he admonished readers. 'Many men are in the habit of going to sleep immediately after coitus; yes, even men who love their wives do this.'

Unbelievable.

Afterplay

Do not cough or sneeze

Aristotle's Works, Containing the Masterpiece. Directions for midwives, counsel and advice to childbearing women, with various useful remedies (London, c. 1860)

When they have done what nature requires, a man must be careful not to withdraw himself from his wife's arms too soon, lest some sudden cold should strike into the womb and occasion miscarriage, and so deprive them of the fruits of their labour.

And when the man has withdrawn himself after a suitable time, the woman should quietly go to rest, with all calmness and composure of mind, free from all anxious and disturbing thoughts, or any other mental worry. And she must, as far as possible, keep from coughing and sneezing, because as it violently shakes the body, it is a great enemy to conception.

Leave her alone

Nicholas Venette, *The Mysteries of Conjugal Love Reveald* (1703)

The wife should not, for three days after, admit the embraces of her husband; to the end that no more seed ... may be added to it.

Stay put

Perfumed Garden of Sheik Nefzaoui (16th century),
translated into English by Sir Richard F. Burton

After the enjoyment is over and your amorous struggle has come to an end, be careful not to get up at
once, but withdraw your member cautiously. Remain
close to the woman, and lie down on the right side of
the bed that witnessed your enjoyment. You will find
this pleasant, and you will not be like a fellow who
mounts the woman after the fashion of a mule, without any regard to refinement, and who, after the
emission, hastens to get his member out, and to rise.
Avoid such manners, for they rob the woman of all
her pleasure.

But –

 Do not drink rain-water directly after
  copulation, because this beverage weakens
  the kidneys.

 Do not work hard directly after coition as this
  might affect your health adversely, but go to
  rest for some time.

 Do not wash your penis directly after having
  withdrawn, until the irritation has gone down
  somewhat; then wash it and its opening
  carefully. Otherwise, do not wash your
  member frequently.

 Do not leave the vulva directly after the
  emission, as this may cause cancer.

Avoid going overboard

Theodoor Hendrik Van de Velde, *Ideal Marriage,
Its Physiology and Technique* (1928)

In afterplay the man proves whether he is (or is not) an erotically civilized adult. This can be so easily done! A word of love will do it, a kiss, a tender touch, an embrace. I confine myself to one suggestion – cultivate this portion of your sexual relation with the greatest care and attention! But at the same time, avoid excess! Extravagance and exaggeration are nowhere more out of place than here, where the imagination requires the utmost delicacy and grace.

Twenty-two

BUY ME AND STOP ONE

America in the 1920s might have been more open than ever before to discussions about sex, but contraception was a different matter.

It was banned, and a tough fight lay in store for anyone who wanted to change that. Step forward Margaret Sanger, women's-rights mercenary (if not quite martyr). Sanger seems to have had a simple ethos: if you are fighting for women, why not use men as munitions?

A short spot of profile-raising incarceration helped her case. In 1917 she was jailed for distributing contraceptive pessaries to immigrant women from a makeshift clinic in Brooklyn. She staged her arrest deliberately to challenge the state's obscenity laws – the legacy of Anthony Comstock, who had died two years earlier, after repeated confrontations with Sanger that won her publicity and support. She was offered a suspended sentence if she promised to uphold the law, but refused and got 30 days' jail. She publicly vowed to go on hunger strike, as her activist sister, Ethel, had done. Once transferred to a more comfortable jail, however, she changed her mind.

Years later, when Hollywood considered a movie of her life, Sanger tried to persuade Ethel to let her rewrite the story so that she, not Ethel, was the hunger-strike heroine.

Sanger was obviously the driven, ambitious sort. But why contraception? The answer lies in her early years. She was born Margaret Louise Higgins into a poor family in 1879. Her mother died at 50, her health wrecked by bearing eleven babies. The young woman's destiny was firmly set in 1913 when, working as a nurse on New York City's Lower East Side, Sanger watched a young patient die from the complications of an illegal abortion. She decided to devote herself to the single-minded pursuit of sexual and reproductive freedom for women. She married at 23 and had three children, but her contraceptive passion became an obsession.

She left her first marriage, to William Sanger, when he began to fail in business. Instead, she committed herself temporarily to free love. Then she married the ageing millionaire J. Noah Slee, the inventor of 3-In-One oil, whom she wooed away from his wife and wed for his money. And what better use for a sugar-daddy than to improve the lot of women worldwide? Slee agreed to use his business to help her to smuggle contraceptives from Europe and also financed her campaigns. When he lost most of his fortune in the Depression, Sanger no longer felt obliged to spend time with him. Her sexual networking did not stop there. One of her many affairs during and after this 22-year marriage was with the writer, H.G. Wells. They shared political beliefs – Wells lobbied for the rational, scientific control of the world's population and helped Sanger get her voice heard at the League of Nations. Handy. She also had an affair with Havelock Ellis and learnt from him how the new popularity of sex manuals might be harnessed for her political ends. Her seductive abilities were helped in no small amount by her looks: she was immensely attractive, small and lithe, with pretty amber-flecked green eyes. H.G. Wells said she had a quick Irish wit, high spirits and radiant common sense – and was 'genuinely pagan'.

With the help of best-selling manuals, she became the Martha Stewart of marital fornication. Through the 1910s and 1920s she wrote popular books, such as *What Every Girl Should Know* and *Happiness in Marriage*, in which she attacked the idea that sex would wear you out: 'Love stimulates the whole glandular system, releases into the body a fresh supply of energy, breaks through the old inhibiting and hindering fears, sweeps aside narrow prim and priggish ideas of life's values, brings new spring to the step, fresh colour to the cheeks, depth and spark to the eye. Love taps an unsuspected and inexhaustible supply of energy which the young lover may convert into ambition and achievement. This is why all the world loves a lover and that is why men and women must learn to remain in love, even though married.' Her soaring prose was highly inspiring – even if that last bit of advice seems a mite hypocritical.

She also published a widely read feminist journal, *The Woman Rebel*, held international conferences,

and lectured extensively in Asia and Europe. Her
ideas do often seem rather mixed up though, a
strange blend of anarchy, free love and the worst
sort of Victorian bigotry. *In What Every Girl Should
Know*, for example, she warns young readers that:
'A girl can waste her creative powers by brooding
over a love affair to the extent of exhausting her
system, with the results not unlike the effects of
masturbation and debauchery.' Worse, she declares:
'The aboriginal Australian, the lowest known
species of the human family, just a step higher than
the chimpanzee in brain development, has so little
sexual control that police authority alone prevents
him from obtaining sexual satisfaction on the
streets.'

Sanger's birth-control movement stalled during
the decades of the Depression and the Second World
War. Without public funding or a new besotted
millionaire to help, the cost and complexity of her
mission proved almost insurmountable. The post-
war years saw the baby boom, when newly wedded
wives dutifully answered the call to be fruitful
and interest in contraception proved low. Sanger
became increasingly irritable and conservative. She
did not help her case by supporting a eugenic drive
for genetic hygiene: she backed the idea of offering
bribes to people with untreatable, disabling genetic
conditions to encourage them to volunteer to be
sterilized. She also wanted tough laws to stop the
'diseased or feebleminded' entering America. In
1950, long after people had witnessed how the logic
of Nazi ideas had led inexorably to the concentration

camps, Sanger was calling for government genetic programmes to bribe married couples with 'defective heredity' to be sterilized.

She turned her attentions abroad. In 1952 she founded the International Planned Parenthood Federation, an umbrella for national associations that remain hard at work today promoting contraception around the world, pressing for women to be granted the fundamental right to control their own bodies. And in her last years, she finally saw progress. A year before she died, the Supreme Court made birth control legal for married couples. When, in September 1966, she died in a Tucson nursing home aged 86, President Lyndon Johnson was beginning to incorporate family planning into America's social-welfare programmes.

How Was It For You?

Six signs of an unsatisfied woman

Kama Sutra of Vatsyayana (3rd century),
translated by Sir Richard F. Burton and F.F. Arbuthnot (1883)

She shakes her hands
She does not let the man get up
She feels dejected
She bites the man
Kicks him
And continues to go on moving after the man
    has finished

Severe congestion

Isobel Emslie Hutton, *The Hygiene of Marriage* (1953)

If the woman does not arrive at orgasm then her sexual organs are left in a state of congestion which may take many hours to pass off. This may result in a more or less chronic state of congestion of the organs with harmful side effects.

Marital injury

Theodoor Hendrik Van de Velde, *Ideal Marriage,
Its Physiology and Technique* (1928)

Every considerable erotic stimulation of wives that does not terminate in orgasm on the woman's part, represents an injury, and repeated injuries of this kind lead to permanent – or very obstinate – damage to both body and soul.

Plus, a nervous breakdown

Marie Stopes, *Married Love* (1918)

The majority of wives are left wakeful and nerve-wracked to watch with tender motherly brooding or with bitter, jealous envy the slumbers of the men who, through ignorance and carelessness have neglected to see that they too had the necessary resolution of nervous tension.

It requires little imagination to see that after months or years of such embittered sleeplessness that a woman tends to become resentful towards her husband. It is to my mind inconceivable that the orgasm in woman as in man should not have profound physiological effects. If we knew enough about the subject, many of the nervous breakdowns and neurotic tendencies of the modern woman could be directly traced to the partial stimulation of sexual intercourse without its normal completion which is so prevalent in modern marriage.

No O? No you

Havelock Ellis, *Analysis of the Sexual Impulse* (1903)

The poor woman who does not get sexual pleasure … has not acquired an erotic personality, she has not mastered the art of life, with the result that her whole nature remains ill-developed and unharmonized, and that she is incapable of bringing her personality – having indeed no achieved personality to bring – to bear effectively on the problems of society and the world around her.

Twenty-three

TARGET FOR TONIGHT

Through the 1930s and 1940s, attitudes in the main continued their steady shuffle towards our present liberal ideas – give or take the odd reactionary writer and barking theorist.

At this point we should salute Dr Helena Wright for helping to bring the clitoris out from under its bushel, finally giving men a clear target for which to aim. Pay attention, chaps: in her 1930 book, *The Sex Factor in Marriage*, she stressed, 'The only purpose of the clitoris is to provide sensation; a full understanding of its capabilities and place in the sex-act is therefore of supreme importance.' For those who failed to heed the message first time round, she stressed in *More about the Sex Factor in Marriage* (1947): 'Since the clitoris is the essential organ of sexual sensation in women, and that rhythmic friction is the only stimulus to which it can react, orgasm failure at the outset of sexual experience is unavoidable if the clitoris is not discovered and correctly stimulated.'

Wright probably inherited her direct sexual approach from her father, a Polish immigrant who became a wealthy British businessman and openly took a new mistress for a year, every year, in order to ensure that the woman never became a threat to his family. In spite of this precaution, Wright's parents divorced when she was a teenager. As an adult, Helena also had an open marriage and enjoyed affairs with younger men. Between the two world wars, she worked in China as a medical missionary, then returned to Britain with a new medical mission – to show her patients where female pleasure lay: 'Women in general take an endless interest in their faces, study them in the mirror and know all their details by heart; but their usual attitude toward their far more important sexual equipment is one of fear and ludicrously complete ignorance,' she wrote in the *Sex Factor in Marriage*. Wright even broached the idea of stimulating a woman through something other than intercourse, thus helping to bust the taboo of masturbation: 'An orgasm induced by the husband's hand, and entirely by way of clitoris sensation, may be a kind and gentle way of introducing a timid and perhaps frightened girl to a happy sex life.'

Her ideas were not all quite so sane. For example, she advised her disciple, Lady Elizabeth Longford, that by douching she could ensure she gave birth to an equal number of sons and daughters. If she wanted a boy, she should use an alkaline douche 30 minutes before intercourse because, Wright claimed, male sperm prefer an alkaline environment. Modern science disagrees. But overall Wright's influence was benign and lasting. Her *Sex, an Outline for Young People,* first published in 1932 as *What Is Sex?,* was still being revised in 1963 and remained on sale in the 1970s.

Not everyone agreed with her pleasure principle. The self-appointed 'medical psychologist' Estelle Cole told her readers that they should ignore the clitoris entirely. In her 1938 book, *Education,* she pushed the nonsensical Freudian idea that proper, emotionally mature women who understood their role in life didn't have silly little clitoral orgasms – they had *vaginal* orgasms, which were big, healthy and clever. Cole wrote: 'A frigid woman is interested in the sensations derived from the stimulation of the clitoris; the vaginal sensations, so necessary for normal and satisfactory intercourse are absent. She has probably been a masturbator and may be unable to rid herself of the habit.' The answer? Get yourself a man, girl.

Leslie Weatherhead was just as much of a re-actionary – and, like Cole, was on a Canute-like campaign to curb the rising tide of Onanism. Weatherhead, a British Methodist minister, claimed that while masturbation was not physically damaging, it could cause psychological harm. But he had a cure (naturally). He was interested in spiritualism, psychic research and hypnotism, and urged patients to use mind-power to master their masturbation. 'Quite recently I have had the joy of curing – apparently completely – a boy who masturbated several times daily for eight years and a girl in whom the practice had been a daily one for nearly 15 years,' he declared. The words 'apparently completely' suggest that even Weatherhead was not convinced.

His mind-power methods ranged from the psychological, urging patients to recognize self-love as 'the misuse on selfish levels of an instinctive energy', to the religious: 'Simply soak the mind with thoughts of Christ.' If those didn't work, there were physical alternatives: circumcision or, less radically, avoiding heavy meals late at night. He also suggested that sufferers sleep with coverings that were 'as light as possible' so as not to heat the lower parts, in a bed that was 'not too soft'. Feather beds, he warned, were wickedness incarnate. His attitude may have been creakingly old fashioned, but Weatherhead's ideas still found a popular market. His *Mastery of Sex through Psychology and Religion* was first published in 1931 and by 1946 had sold 70,000 copies in 15 editions.

The award for sanest pre-war advice must go to the husband-and-wife team, Hannah and Abraham Stone, for their soberly titled, *A Marriage Manual.* It oozed sensibleness, disguising its quietly progressive opinions behind an authoritative black cover. The Stones had worked with Margaret Sanger to popularize birth control, but firmly rejected her beloved idea of compulsory sterilization for so-called defectives, calling it 'a dangerous social policy'. Nevertheless such sterilization was actually permitted or even ordered at the time in 30 American states.

The pair set up America's first official marriage-consultation service and pioneered ways of working with couples and groups – an approach which became increasingly popular in the wake of the Second World War, when vast numbers of servicemen's marriages threatened to disintegrate after years of enforced separation. Their book was written using a similar approach, as a dialogue between a doctor and a young couple about to be married, echoing once again the Q&A format of humankind's very first written advice.

The *Marriage Manual* was widely lauded by critics for its practical and down-to-earth advice. The public loved it, and the text was reprinted 22 times between its publication in 1935 and 1952. It introduced the practice of scattering health texts with 'pertinent facts' ... did you know that, apparently, the clitoris was first named by a man called Columbus (albeit not Christopher)? Other sex facts were backed by the Stones' own research, such as measuring the distance from vagina to clitoris in a sample of patients (results: from 0.5in to 2.5in). Given the times and political climes in which they worked, the Stones were paragons of reason. But not completely: they rejected normal intercourse from the rear, saying it was unromantic and used 'only among certain primitive peoples'.

Hannah died young, at 46, after which Abraham, a short, dark Russian-born man with a moustache, continued their work promoting contraception and marital therapy. After he retired, he spent his last years raising cows and chickens on a farm in New Jersey and ice-skating.

Beware of Celibacy

Boils and ulcers

Fang-nei-pu-I (*Healthy Sex Life*), by the
Taoist physician Sun Szu-mo (AD 601–682)

Man's passion naturally has its periods of great abundance. Therefore even superior men cannot bear a protracted abstention from sexual intercourse. If a man abstains too long from emitting semen, he will develop boils and ulcers. But if a strong man of over 60 feels that his thoughts are still composed after not having copulated with a woman for one month or so, then he can afford not to engage in sexual intercourse any longer.

As a rule, forcible suppression of the urge is difficult to attain and easy to lose again. It will cause a man to suffer from involuntary emissions and turgid urine, finally leading to his being haunted by incubi. One emission of semen will then equal the loss caused by a hundred emissions of a man who leads a normal sex life.

Overwork

Havelock Ellis, *Psychology of Sex:
a manual for students* (1933)

The difficulties of sexual abstinence, even though they do not involve any great risk to life or to sanity, are still very real to many healthy and active persons. It is apt to cause minor disturbances of physical wellbeing, and on the psychic side much mental worry and a constantly recurring struggle with erotic obsessions, an unwholesome sexual hyperaesthesia which, especially in women, often takes on the form of prudery.

A student, for instance, who lives chastely, who is ambitious, who wishes to put all his best energies into his studies, may endure great anxiety and mental depression from this struggle. Many young women, also, actively engaged in various kinds of work, suffer similarly and are sometimes stimulated to a feverish activity in work and physical exercise which usually brings no relief.

Nerves and fibroids

Marie Stopes, *Married Love* (1918)

The medical man can produce an imposing list of diseases more or less directly caused by abstinence both in men and women. These diseases range from neuralgia and 'nerves' (in women) to fibroid growths. And it is well worthy of remark that these diseases may be present when the patient (as in many unmarried women) has no idea that the sex-impulse exists unmastered.

Evil spinster syndrome

George Riley Scott, *Your Sex Questions Answered* (1947)

Sex is a biological need in a woman's life as it is in a man's. It is a fact so noteworthy as to rank almost as a platitude that the middle-aged spinster is unhappy, bad-tempered and so psychologically abnormal that she is difficult to live with ... the reason for the evolution of this type of mind is sex repression.

How to cure a celibate woman

Havelock Ellis, *Psychology of Sex: a manual for students* (1933)

The main part of the task of curing sexual anaesthesia in a woman must usually rest with her husband. He is by no means always equipped for this treatment. One fears that there is still too much truth in Balzac's saying that in this matter the husband is sometimes like an orang-utang with a violin.

It must be admitted that the husband's task is often difficult. The difficulty is increased by the late age at which in civilisation a woman enters the state of marriage after a long period of years in which she has presumably been leading a life of chastity.

During those long years there has been, we know, a constant generation of sexual energy which must be consumed along some channel or other. The woman has acquired habits and fallen into routines. Her whole nervous system has been moulded and hardened. Even on the physical side of sex, the organs are by no means always so ready to respond normally to the exercise of their natural functions.

Why girls get cold feet

Aristotle's Works, Containing the Masterpiece. Directions for midwives, counsel and advice to childbearing women, with various useful remedies (London, c. 1860)

The natural end of man and women's being is to propagate. Now in the act of conception, there must be an agent and patient; for if they be both every way of one constitution they cannot propagate: man therefore is hot and dry, woman cold and moist; he is the agent, she the patient or weaker vessel, that she should be subject to the office of the man.

It is necessary the woman should be of a cold constitution, because in her is required a redundancy of nature for the infant depending up on her; for otherwise, if there were not a surplus of nourishment for the child, more than is convenient for the mother, then would the infant detract and weaken the principal parts of the mother, and like unto the viper, the generating of the infant would be the destruction of the parent.

Twenty-four

FRIGID FIFTIES

The march of sexual liberation rather stubbed its toe on the post-war years.

The trauma of mass wartime destruction and displacement in Europe was followed by years of grim austerity, where food, shelter and normality took priority over free love. By contrast, America's industrial boom showered its folk with unprecedented material riches, creating a society paralysed by the rictus grin of its own apparent success: happy husbands, permed wives and Stepford sex.

After the Second World War, popular manuals tended to give priority to men's pleasure. This is what passed as sex advice in *Esquire* magazine: 'First date: Camellias. They're less usual than gardenias. First surprise: sewing machine or a wash tub. If she's bright, she'll catch on.' If women wanted a happy marriage, they were expected to ensure that marital sex appeared successful. Even if they didn't actually enjoy the experience, they could still lie back and think of kitchen appliances. Women who refused to fake it found themselves described as emotionally and psychologically deficient, suffering from frigidity, prudishness and neurosis. Eustace Chesser's *Love Without Fear*, which was first published in 1941 and beat an American censorship attempt the following year, proved highly popular through the 1950s and promoted the idea that good marital sex should involve both parties orgasming – but it also suggested if the woman didn't come she might be better off looking as though she had.

Joan Malleson put her finger on the problem in 1950 when she published *Any Wife or Any Husband*, saying 'Many wives are aware that the full use of the outer clitoral area will alone bring them satisfaction, yet they are too afraid to ask their husbands to touch this part of their body in the proper way.' Perhaps these wives were afraid that they might receive a response inspired by Edward Podolsky's contemporary *Sex Technique for Husband and Wife*, in which he declared 'The clitoris, while important, is not nearly as important as many of us have been taught or led to believe.'

Podolsky typified the prevailing approach: women should be compliant, grateful – and, in particular, undemanding. He even created a new disorder – 'exaggerated sexual craving' – to describe wives who fancied intercourse more often than their husbands did. Podolsky's 1942 *Modern Sex Manual* warned that this morbid condition had become a curse that doctors faced helplessly every day: 'Mental treatment, or psychotherapy, has been tried, but the results are negligible. Simply telling a woman to exert some willpower to control her abnormal sex craving is not enough,' he warned.

Oddly enough, these unreasonable sexual demands seemed to go hand-in-hand with the woman patients becoming overweight and post-menopausal – and thus very possibly less desirable. We can guess, too, that this might coincide with hubby's own libido flagging. Wifey wanting sex was suddenly a medical terror.

Fortunately, Podolsky had the answer: 'With startling advances in female hormonology, this problem is well on the way toward solution. The new remedy is the male sex hormone, testosterone,' he wrote. 'It is injected once every two days and relief is obtained. In some there is a recurrence of the morbid sex craving.' Exactly what testosterone did to these women is open to question. Perhaps they grew moustaches, developed an interest in beer, fast cars and baseball – and left their husbands alone. Horny women became an official medical problem: in 1951, nymphomania was defined as a sexual deviation in America's first formal attempt to categorize psychiatric illness: the *Diagnostic and Statistical Manual of Mental Disorders*. Three years later, the idea of female sexuality became a literary problem, too. Gustave Flaubert's 1857 novel *Madame Bovary* was placed on the blacklist of the U.S. National Organization of Decent Literature for depicting a woman driven by sexual desire. The character Emma is married to a small-town doctor but takes a rich landowner and a legal clerk as lovers. Flaubert's doctor obviously hadn't heard of testosterone.

The gates of progress had not warped completely shut, however. Alfred Kinsey's anecdotally based reports on ordinary Americans' sex lives offered some opportunity to discuss the matter openly – though much of that discussion consisted of vitriolic attacks on Kinsey. (Much the same happened in 1966 when William Masters and Virginia Johnson described their laboratory observations of what happens when you put a naked man on top of a naked woman. They were inundated by hate mail, which outnumbered supportive letters by nine to one.)

Don't Overdo It

The ruin of thousands

Nicholas de Venette,
Tableau de l'amour conjugal (1696)

Unbounded licentiousness in the conduct of the marriage bed is the ruin of many thousand couples. It is like bathing in cold water which, if sparingly exercised, recruits the strength, but if too often had recourse to, enervates and destroys it.

It borders on criminal

John Harvey Kellogg,
Plain Facts for Old And Young (1877)

Many a man has, until his marriage, lived a most continent life; so has his wife. As soon as they are wedded, intercourse is indulged in night after night, neither party having any idea that these repeated sexual acts are excesses which the system of neither can bear, and which, to the man at least, are absolute ruin. The practice is continued till health is impaired, sometimes permanently; and when a patient is at last obliged to seek medical advice, he is thunderstruck at learning that his sufferings arise from excesses unwittingly committed. Till they are told of the danger, the idea never enters their heads that they are guilty of great and almost criminal excess.

It's depressing

William Chidley, *The Answer* (1912)

The high degree of nervous excitement which the act of coition involves produces a depression of spirits to a corresponding amount, and the too frequent repetition of it is productive of consequences very injurious to the general health.

Women steal your strength

Albertus Magnus, *De Secretis Mulierum* (*The Secrets of Women*) (c. 1478)

Too much ejaculation dries out the body because the sperm has the power of humidifying and heating. That is why men who copulate too much and too often do not live long.

The more women have sexual intercourse, the stronger they become, because they are made hot by the motion that the man makes during coitus. Further, male sperm is hot because it is of the same nature as air and when it is received by the woman it warms her entire body, so women are strengthened by this heat. On the other hand, men who have sex frequently are weakened by this act because they become exceedingly dried out.

Your skin will flake

Giovanni Marinello, *Medicine Pertinent to the Infirmities of Women* (Italy, 1563)

Symptoms of overindulgence:

General weakness
Loss of vision
Loss of memory
Pallid complexion
Flaky skin
Yellow or brown spots

You'll become gullible ...

Nicholas Venette, *The Mysteries of Conjugal Love Reveald* (1703)

If a man too far indulges himself in these pleasures, and especially in his youth gives way to frequent coition, it will cross his present health, debilitate his generative faculties and entirely subvert his constitution ... he becomes slow in action, heavy in gait, dull in his conversation, stupid in his comprehension, unadvised in his labour and apt to believe everything; the hair of the head will fall off or grow quickly grey ... his life will be shortened two-thirds of its date.

– but strong wine up the nose will fix it

Let me advise those who have injured their health by the immoderate use of women to wash their nostrils, their wrists and the palms of their hands with the strongest-bodied wine they can get; which though a simple remedy, may be attended with very salutary effects.

No one loves an overweight nympho

Edward Podolsky, *Modern Sex Manual* (1942)

For many years the treatment and management of exaggerated sexual craving in women has been a problem which many physicians and psychiatrists have had to face in daily consultation. Typically, the problem arises during the menopause and is accompanied by a sudden increase in weight, which is directly related to the sexual craving. Frankly there was actually very little that could be done.

With startling advances in female hormonology this problem is well on the way toward solution. The new remedy is, strangely enough, the male sex hormone ... It is injected once every two days and relief is obtained. In some there is a recurrence of the morbid sex craving.

Do something creative instead

Marie Stopes, *Married Love* (1918)

Analysis of the chemical nature of the ejaculated fluid reveals among other things a remarkably high percentage of calcium and phosphoric acid – both precious substances in our organization. It is therefore the greatest mistake to imagine that semen is something to be got rid of frequently – all the vital energy and nerve-force involved in its ejaculation and the precious chemical substances which go to its composition can be better utilized by being transformed into other creative work on most days of the month.

Or be a boy scout

Robert Baden-Powell,
Rovering to Success (1922)

Sex is not everything in life, and other energies take the place of sex and relieve the strain. The energy that the primitive male animal puts almost solely into sex, in the human is turned into all sorts of other activities such as art, science and a hundred and one other things. So the more interests you have and the more you follow them with keenness, the less will primitive sex urges worry you … Now you can see how Rovering comes in. Instead of aimless loafing and smutty talks you will find lots to do in the way of hiking and enjoyment of the out-of-door manly activities. Without knowing it you are putting something in the place of sex.

241

Live to make love at 70

Nicholas Venette, *The Mysteries of Conjugal Love Reveald* (1703)

If moderation is of use in any thing, it ought, without doubt, to be so in the embraces of women ... an old man of seventy will be in a condition to caress a young woman and get children, if he has not taken too much liberty with the ladies during his youth.

When a man gives himself up to lust, he loses his plumpness and good air; his head grows bald, his eyes tarnished and livid and the fire which formerly was perceived is then vanished.

The brain, which is the principal organ of all faculties of the soul, cools and dries by the loss of humours we sustain in caresses of women. In some lascivious men it is no bigger than one's fist. The eyes grow sad and hollow through the scarcity of the spirits, the cheeks thin, the forehead withered and callous, the hearing become hard, the breath stinking.

Twenty-five

SAUCY SIXTIES

The early Sixties were anything but uniformly swinging.

The 1964 *Newnes Manual of Marriage*, for example, firmly slapped down any thoughts of pre-marital sex or even an exploratory fondle, declaring: 'It can be said with confidence that any manipulation of the genital organs is overstepping the mark and these might well be thought to include the breasts.' But social progress began steadily to head in one direction. Consumerist opinion-leaders, particularly the big Madison Avenue advertising agencies, discovered that they could sell many more products by encouraging people to think of themselves as rebellious individuals, rather than convention-hugging nice guys. The surge in self-awareness this fostered resulted neatly in people wanting to buy more goods that expressed their 'unique identity' and sense of freedom. These new approaches inevitably washed into the world of sex, too.

The radical change in attitudes was helped by a technological breakthrough – the Pill, which was licensed by America's Food and Drug Administration in 1960. It gave women a greater sense of sexual freedom than any previous contraceptive, thus helping plenty of men to get laid more often. In Britain and America, D.H. Lawrence's classic 1926 sex story *Lady Chatterley's Lover* was finally legalized after winning showpiece trials on both sides of the Atlantic. This encouraged publishers to blow the dust off other long-banned old texts, including Sir Richard Burton's translation of the *Kama Sutra*. And in 1961, an English expert in elderly people's medicine produced a scholarly translation of another Indian sex manual, the medieval *Koka Shastra*. Its publication date of 1963 was, for the poet Philip Larkin, the year in which sexual intercourse began, betwixt 'the end of the Chatterley ban and the Beatles' first LP'.

The nudge-nudge notoriety of anything Oriental that mentioned sex ensured the *Koka Shastra* sold well in Britain. This gave ample encouragement to its translator, a certain Dr Alex Comfort, who was soon to become the seventies' hippy humping guru with his book *The Joy of Sex*. The *Koka Shastra*'s twelfth-century text, ironically, was a backlash against the free-sex attitudes of the earlier *Kama Sutra*. Medieval India had witnessed a moral clampdown. Instead of encouraging readers to have multiple partners, the *Koka Shastra* said its sex advice was an aid to monogamy: 'The husband, by varying the enjoyment of his wife, may live with her as with 32 different women, ever varying the enjoyment of her and rendering satiety impossible.'

Comfort wrote a long academic introduction to the book, but closed it with a plea from the heart. 'Dare one hope that the next echelon of sex-advice literature, with the advantages behind it of science, biology, psychology, experience and, most important of all, a civilized and guilt-free view of sexuality as pleasure and fulfilment, may come eventually from our own culture? It seems quite possible, if the present weather holds.'

The weather did more than hold. It began to brew a sex-manual storm. In 1962, Helen Gurley Brown published *Sex and the Single girl: the unmarried woman's guide to men, careers, the apartment, diet, fashion, money and men*. The title itself would have been unthinkable a decade earlier, and so would the advice: readers shouldn't feel guilty about having sex, they would be lunatics not to bed-test potential husbands and, in the absence of eligible bachelors, married men would sometimes have to do. By April 1963, it had sold 150,000 hardcover copies. When Gurley Brown took over the editorship of *Cosmopolitan* in 1965, she effectively turned the magazine into a monthly glossy lifestyle manual that either empowered readers or left them feeling sorely inadequate. Many other magazines followed suit.

There was much more to come. In 1969, Joan Garrity, identifying herself only as 'J', wrote *The Way to Become the Sensuous Woman*, complete with tongue exercises and masturbation tips. The book was written on a publisher's whim after Garrity had written a cut-price guide to New York and was working as a publicist at their office. The chapter on self-pleasure caused the biggest stir: 'To awaken your body and make it perform well, you must train like an athlete for the act of love,' she wrote. Seventeen years later, Garrity remembered, 'In those days, women wanted to have orgasms and never knew how. I put it in the first person so it could be cozy. And I wrote it in very simple language, so all women could understand it.'

The formula worked: in its first year in print it attracted 13 million readers and earned $1 million. In 1971, however, things turned sour when Garrity sued her publisher, claiming unpaid royalties, and in 1984 she co-authored the *Story of 'J': the author of* The sensuous woman *tells the bitter price of her crazy success*. In 1988 she turned up in a Palm Beach suburb, an insomniac overweight gardening fan who hosted a morning phone-in show for a local radio station.

1969 also saw the appearance of the psychiatrist Dr David Reuben's book *Everything You Always Wanted to Know about Sex (but were afraid to ask)*. Around 100 million people have now read it, but initially the book failed to find a publisher. His original proposal for a humorous sex manual titled, *Beyond the Birds and Bees* was rejected more than 20 times. One publisher sent him a note saying, 'Funny books about sex close on Saturday night.' But it finally got printed – and the marketing proved brilliant. The publisher had chosen the new title, with just the right level of wit. The book's brave, bright-yellow cover appealed to booksellers, and its timing was excellent. And although the book's sexual descriptions were highly detailed, it did not feature explicit images. Booksellers weren't quite ready for that yet. *Life* magazine and the *New York Times* both gave it good reviews and sales began to soar. To a post-war generation that would never believe that Van de Velde's Edwardian manual or Kellogg's Victorian anti-masturbation rant could ever have been bestsellers, it looked like the Age of Aquarius had chalked up another revolution. In fact, it simply meant that sex books were back on top again, and were just as odd as ever.

Reuben neatly updated the ancient Chinese sex manuals' question-and-answer format to cover questions such as 'What is the average penis size?' and 'When does someone actually get too old for sex?' It was a number-one hit in 51 countries, despite the fact that Reuben's jovial writing style was neither elegant nor entirely accurate. Some of the advice was seriously awry – 'orgasm usually brings on a lapse of consciousness' ... 'LSD is an aphrodisiac' ... and preferring oral sex to inter-course is 'a probable sign of an emotional problem'. Reuben recommended Coca-Cola as 'the best douche available'. Doctors warned it was so danger-ous it could cause peritonitis. In 1972, a *Playboy* article pointed out a hundred errors.

The book inspired Woody Allen to direct a 1972 film of the same name, in which each sketch is derived from one of Reuben's questions: do aphro-disiacs work? what is sodomy? and why do some women have trouble reaching orgasm? But Reuben's text became increasingly derided for its inveterate squareness: cross-dressing and pornography were perversions, and while heterosexual sadomasochists were 'like timid children playing games', gay sadomasochists were 'among the cruellest people who walk this earth'. The homophobia was rabid. Reuben wrote that gay men are condemned to a miserable life of questing for something they cannot have. He added that the vast majority of homosexual encounters are impersonal, 'No feeling, no sentiment, no nothing ... a masturbation machine might do it better.' In a massively revised 1999 reprint he added an 'Important note' that effectively retracted these statements, but he had received a massive rebuttal only three years after the book first came out – in the form of Alex Comfort's *The Joy of Sex*.

You'll go blind – or worse . . .

Masturbation: the causes

Stanley G. Hall, *Adolescence* (1911)

Springtime, warm climates, improper clothes, rich food, indigestion, mental overwork, nervousness, habits of defective cleanliness, especially of a local kind, prolonged sitting or standing, too monotonous walking, sitting cross-legged, spanking, late rising, petting and indulgence, corsets that produce stagnation or hyperaemia of blood in the lower part of the body and too great straining of the memory.

Blame it on the banisters

Sylvanus Stall, *What Young Boys Ought to Know* (1905)

Many pure-minded and innocent boys have learned the habit in very innocent ways, and in the beginning not even mistrusting that the habit was either wicked or injurious. Many boys at a very early age have discovered the sensation by sliding down the banisters, or at a little later period in life by climbing and descending trees, by riding on horse-back, and some because of uncleanness of the sexual member have experienced an itching of these parts, and when relief has been sought by chafing or rubbing, the child has been introduced to the habit of self-pollution.

And white-collar work

Dr Frederick Hollick, *The Male Generative Organs in Health and Disease, from Infancy to Old Age* (c. 1845)

Figures from the annual reports of the Massachusetts State Lunatic Asylum show that ...

Light sedentary employments very much favour the formation of solitary vice, and on the contrary, active out-of-door occupation has the contrary effect. Thus among merchants, printers, students and shoemakers, 50 per cent of the insanity arises from masturbation, and only 12 per cent from intemperance; while among carpenters, blacksmiths and others who are actively employed, 35 per cent of the insanity arises from intemperance and only 13 per cent from masturbation ... These facts should be duly weighed by parents when choosing employment for their sons.

Single-handed victims

John Marten, *Treatise of all the Symptoms of the Venereal Disease* (1709)

With meagre jaws and pale looks, seldom without scabs and blotches, those loathsome relicts of their odious vices, with limber hams, and legs without calves, feeble at mature years, as rickety children, weak and consumptive, when they should by nature be most hail and vigorous; rotten before they are full ripe, and fit for nothing in the prime of their years but to be lodged in an hospital.

Is your child guilty? Danger signs

John Harvey Kellogg,
Plain Facts for Old and Young (1877)

General debility
Early symptoms of tuberculosis
Premature and defective development
Lassitude
Sleeplessness
Failure of mental capacity
Fickleness
Untrustworthiness
Love of solitude
Bashfulness
Unnatural boldness
Mock piety
Timidity
Round shoulders and stooping posture
Weak backs and pains in the limbs and stiffness
    of the joints
Paralysis of the lower extremities
Strange gait
Lack of development in the breasts of females
Capricious appetite
The use of tobacco
Acne or pimples
Biting the fingernails – very common in girls
An habitually cold, moist hand
Hysteria in females
Epileptic fits
Wetting the bed

Is your child an Onanist? The signs (again)

Stanley G. Hall, *Adolescence* (1911)

Optical cramps, goitre, intensification of the patellar reflex, weak sluggishness of heart action and circulation, cold extremities, purple and dry skin, lassitude and flaccidity, clammy hands, anaemic complexion, dry cough and many digestive perversions, listlessness and frigidity, a predisposition to convulsions, early signs of decrepitude and senescence. Gray hairs and especially baldness, a stooping and enfeebled gait.

More signs of self-sex

Dr Henry Guernsey,
Plain Talks on Avoided Subjects (1882)

Look at the habitual masturbator! See how thin, pale and haggard he appears; how his eyes are sunken; how long and cadaverous is his cast of countenance; how irritable he is and how sluggish, mentally and physically; how afraid he is to meet the eye of his fellow, feel his damp and chilling hand, so characteristic of great vital exhaustion.

It kills women

Fang Nei Chi (Records of the Bedchamber),
Sui Dynasty (AD 590–618)

Some women are fond of masturbating by inserting a small pouch filled with grain or an ivory rod into their vaginas. All such instruments for artificial satisfaction are robbers of life. They will cause a woman to grow old quickly and die before her time.

Turns boys into mouth-rotted idiots

Robert Baden-Powell, *Scouting for Boys*
(uncut, 1908)

The practice is called self abuse and the result is that the boy after time becomes weak and nervous and shy. He gets headaches and probably palpitation of the heart, and if he still carries it on too far he very often goes out of his mind and becomes an idiot … Remember too that several awful diseases come from indulgence – one especially that rots away the inside of men's mouths, their noses and eyes.

Paraphymosis? Don't ask

Onania, or the heinous sin of self-pollution, and all its frightful consequences, in both sexes, considered: with spiritual and physical advice to those who have already injured themselves by this abominable practice (1712)

Self-pollution manifestly hinders the growth, both in girls and boys, and few of either sex that in their youth commit this sin to excess for any considerable time, come ever to that robustness or strength which they would have arrived to without it. In men, as well as boys, the first attempt of it has often occasioned a Phymosis in some, and a Paraphymosis in others: I shall not explain these terms any further; let it suffice, that they are accidents which are very painful and troublesome.

Menstrual derangement

Our Family Physician: a manual for home usage; allopathic, hydropathic, eclectic, & herbal (1871)

Some of the consequences of masturbation are epilepsy, apoplexy, paralysis, premature old age, involuntary discharge of seminal fluid, which generally occurs during sleep, or after urinating, or when evacuating the bowels. Among females, besides these other consequences, we have hysteria, menstrual derangement, catalepsy and strange nervous symptoms.

Head decay?

Appeal to Mothers (1864),
by the Seventh Day Adventist prophet Ellen G. White

Masturbators will suffer: affection of the liver and lungs, neuralgia, rheumatism, affection of the spine, diseased kidneys, and cancerous humours, catarrh, dropsy, headache, loss of memory and sight, great weakness in the back and loins, affections of the spine, the head often decays inwardly. The mind is often utterly ruined, and insanity takes place.

... and finally suicide

*Onania, or the heinous sin of self-pollution, and all its frightful
consequences, in both sexes, considered: with spiritual and physical
advice to those who have already injured themselves by this
abominable practice* (1712)

Disturbances of the stomach and digestion, loss of appetite or ravenous hunger, vomiting, nausea, weakening of the organs of breathing, coughing, hoarseness, paralysis, weakening of the organ of generation to the point of impotence, lack of libido, back pain, disorders of the eye and ear, total diminution of bodily powers, paleness, thinness, pimples on the face, decline of intellectual powers, loss of memory, attacks of rage, madness, idiocy, epilepsy, fever and finally suicide.

A cure! (maybe)

Sylvanus Stall, *What Young Boys Ought to Know* (1905)

Boys often have to be put in a 'straitjacket', sometimes have their hands fastened behind their backs, sometimes their hands are tied to the posts of the bed, or fastened by ropes or chains to rings in the wall; and in various other ways extreme measures have to be resorted to in the effort to save the person from total mental and physical self-destruction. And I am sorry to say that even these extreme measures are not always successful in restraining them or effecting a cure.

Or worse …

John Harvey Kellogg,
Plain Facts for Old and Young (1877)

A remedy for masturbation which is almost always successful in small boys is circumcision. The operation should be performed by a surgeon without administering an anaesthetic, as the brief pain attending the operation will have a salutary effect upon the mind, especially if it be connected with the idea of punishment. In females, the author has found the application of pure carbolic acid to the clitoris an excellent means of allaying the abnormal excitement.

Twenty-six

COMFORT AND JOY

Comfort's book wrote the manifesto for our new, sex-sodden age, when he declared: 'In books prior to the seventies, perversion meant, quite simply, any sexual behaviour which the writer himself did not enjoy.'

Comfort declared that people should worry less about harmless sexual quirks, and more about 'the commonest perversions in our culture ... getting hold of some power and using it to kick other people around, money-hunting as a status activity, treating other people, sexually or otherwise, as things to manipulate and interfering with other people's sex lives'. Right on, man. *The Joy of Sex* was not only the first sexually explicit illustrated sex manual to be widely published. It was also the hairiest: bushy beard, legs, armpits, everything. Comfort even embraced promiscuity, unlike Reuben. He was in favour of steady relationships – but said they can last 50 years or 15 minutes. He was also sympathetic to gays and lesbians.

It was the first manual to treat sexual activity purely as pleasure, with headings such as 'gadgets and gimmicks' or 'foursomes and moresomes' and a gourmet approach to coupling that relied on sensual culinary descriptions. It was nothing short of a phenomenon. Since 1972, it has sold more than 12 million copies, been translated into two dozen languages and reportedly earned $3 million for the author. But Comfort described *The Joy of Sex* as an 'albatross' that detracted from his other contributions to science and the arts. In his long and productive life, he wrote 50 other texts, ranging from a novel about the Roman Emperor Nero, to medical textbooks and volumes of poetry. But everyone remembers him as the free-love freak who wrote that hippy manual.

That's what you get for being a troublemaker. He was born in 1920 in North London and began causing chaos at an early age. Comfort described himself during childhood as a 'perfect little bastard'. He blew the fingers off his left hand at the age of 14 while trying to make gunpowder. After running away from school, his mother taught him from their home. But his literary promise was evident early on, too. Comfort wrote his first book, *The Silver River*, when he was only 18. He based it on a trip he took with his father to Africa and South America. Newspaper reviewers praised his precocious talent.

His hippy tendencies showed themselves as a young man in the Second World War, when he declared himself a conscientious objector. Instead of fighting, he studied medicine at Trinity College, Cambridge, but failed his medical finals the first time round because, having emerged from an air-raid shelter dirty, unshaven and scruffy, the patient he was to examine refused to let him near them. A medical career was not enough, though, and the young Dr Comfort turned to writing poetry, becoming lauded as one of Britain's most promising young poets. After the war he joined the Campaign for Nuclear Disarmament and ran a pirate ban-the-bomb radio station, using a mobile transmitter to interrupt BBC news bulletins with his anarchist propaganda. He was never caught. Comfort also wrote a popular protest song that was adopted by Nina Simone. Considering his later claim to fame, it had the unlikely title of *Go Limp* – an instruction to peace marchers on how to resist arrest passively.

In 1960, he joined the Committee of 100, which had been launched by the philosopher Bertrand Russell to organize mass civil disobedience against Britain's nuclear arsenal. The following year, he was jailed for a month with around 40 other committee members for refusing to be bound over to keep the peace. His fellow prisoners included some of the era's leading creative minds, such as the playwright Robert Bolt. Comfort spent some of his jail time teaching his cellmate, the 89-year-old Russell, to sing Irish revolutionary songs. Comfort was also among the great and good who wrote an open letter to *The Times* in 1967, supporting the Wolfenden Report's call for gay sex to be legalized.

Comfort's medical career prospered despite his activism. He lectured in physiology and then specialized in gerontology – elderly people's medicine – at University College, London. He discovered the life-prolonging powers of artificial antioxidants and his 1956 book *The Biology of Senescence* remains a seminal work on ageing. He continued to write – poetry, novels, social histories and literary criticism. In 1961, his *Darwin and the Naked Lady* reminded the world of the power of Indian erotica, and three years later, his *Koka Shastra* translation hit the shelves.

Comfort dismissively remembered writing *The Joy of Sex: a gourmet guide to lovemaking*, in only two weeks. 'Somebody rang me to say that the London Hospital was not teaching sex properly and would I talk to them about it. So I spoke to the head of professional psychiatry and ended up agreeing to write a book myself,' he recalled. He denied, somewhat disingenuously, ever being any kind of authority on sex before he wrote the book. He claimed he did the research while he was doing the writing. On another occasion he claimed the book was based on a mix of personal experience, reading and talking to people. Perhaps, though, the book wrote itself, thanks to experience learnt from his complicated personal life. Comfort had attempted to pioneer dual-domesticity – living with two women in two different houses. He called them Wife 1 and Wife 2, but the experiment failed and he was forced to choose between them. Shortly after *The Joy of Sex* was published, his 29-year marriage to Ruth Muriel Harris ended in divorce and he married Wife 2, the sociologist Jane Henderson.

The book was originally called *Cordon Bleu Sex*, but the owners of the Cordon Bleu copyright objected. The replacement title was possibly inspired by a contemporary Buddhist book, *Joy*, but remained modelled on gourmet cooking. The book was arranged in three sections, 'Starters', 'Main courses' and 'Sauces and pickles'. Its jaunty style also helped to distance it neatly from the tawdry world of porno. Sex, just like food, was now lifestyle. 'Chef-grade cooking doesn't happen naturally,' Comfort wrote. 'It's hard to make mayonnaise by trial and error, for instance. Cordon Bleu sex, as we define it, is exactly the same situation.' And if you had a mishap with the mayonnaise, the book included practical advice such as how to remove stains – 'with a stiff brush, when the stain has dried, or with a dilute solution of sodium bicarbonate'.

It was written with the simple aim, Comfort said, of showing that sex could be fun. There was a political motive, too: he believed that sexually fulfilled lovers were unlikely to harm others, saying: 'If people have a very happy home life, as I've always had, they are probably extremely reluctant to kill people they have never met. War is for mugs.'

Soon after the book was published, Comfort moved to California and lectured in psychiatry at Stanford University. Later he became a professor at the University of California at Berkeley's neuro-psychiatric institute. He also joined the Sandstone experimental sexual community in Topanga Canyon near Los Angeles, which he wrote about in his best-selling follow-up, *More Joy of Sex*. Gay Talese, an American writer, visited Sandstone in the early 1970s, and in his 1981 book *Thy Neighbor's Wife*, described him. 'Often the nude biologist, brandishing a cigar, traipsed through the room between the prone bodies with the professional air of a lepidopterist strolling through the fields waving a butterfly net. A gray-haired, bespectacled owlish man with a well-preserved body, Dr Comfort was unabashedly drawn to the sight of sexually engaged couples. With the least amount of encouragement – after he had deposited his cigar in a safe place – he would join the friendly clutch of bodies and contribute to the merriment.'

Comfort said he did not recognize the description and, indeed, according to his journalist son Nick, life with Dr Joy as his father proved to be a distinctly erogenous-free zone: 'His idea of sex education was to race through the most basic facts of life when I was 12 – and then only after my school had sent him a missive about personal hygiene,' Nick wrote. 'It is the disappointing truth that, while life with a father of staggeringly varied intellectual interests was seldom dull, I probably heard less talk about sex than the average child.'

Comfort died on 26 March 2000 at a nursing home in Britain, aged 80, after a series of strokes. The philosophy of his early poems ruled his work. In 1946, he had written, 'I recognize two obligations: to do nothing to increase the total of human suffering, and to leave nothing undone which diminishes it.' In 1994, he declared that he still held these principles, 'But I've become more of a Buddhist.'

Keep Your Woman Faithful

Use monkey poo

Kama Sutra of Vatsyayana (3rd century),
translated by Sir Richard F. Burton and F.F. Arbuthnot (1883)

If a man mixes the powder of the milk hedge plant and the kantaka plant with the excrement of a monkey and the powdered root of the lanjalika plant, and throws this mixture on a woman, she will not love anybody else afterwards.

Or try birdshit

Ratimanjari of Jayadeva (*The Posy of Love*)
(India, *c.* 16th century)

If a man has commerce with a woman, having first rubbed his member with dung dropped by a valguli-bird in flight, she will never have anything to do with any other man.

How to cheat yo' man

Aristotle's Works, Containing the Masterpiece. Directions for midwives, counsel and advice to childbearing women, with various useful remedies (London c. 1860)

Nothing is more powerful than the imagination of the mother; for if she fix her eyes upon any object it will so impress her mind, that it often happens that the child has a representation thereof on some part of the body. If in act of copulation, the woman earnestly look on the man, and fix her mind on him, the child will resemble its father. Nay, if a woman, even in unlawful copulation, fix her mind upon her husband, the child will resemble him though he did not beget it.

Twenty-seven

SEX AS LIFESTYLE

Comfort's death marks the end of a breed, and thus the end of this history. Why stop here?

It is not simply because Dr Joy was the last in a long and eccentric line of true misfit manual writers, but also because his work finally brought us full-circle back to the original Chinese manuals' unabashed accent on sexual pleasure – albeit in the interests of peace and love, rather than immortality. *The Joy of Sex* also put copulation back on top of the coffee table, rather than under the counter, as an activity that was healthy rather than a cause of deep, disabling shame. Irwin Edman predicted with surprising accuracy in 1932 that, 'By 1982 sex will have become much less a theme for either poetry or analysis. Much of the romanticism and all of the hypochondria on the subject will be over.' Perhaps, though, he could have more accurately swapped romanticism with hypochondria.

The book also ends here in order to evade a diffi-cult and perplexing question: how do you examine today's overcrowded advice market? The question is akin to asking, how do you study a stampede? The clamour of sex advice that now comes at us from more angles than a Roman orgy is notable more for its volume than its content. It is, in its everything-goes, self-help, live-your-life style, ultimately homo-genized, and driven infinitely more by marketing budgets and focus groups than by the eccentric whims of social outcasts and dreamers. That is not to deny that it is a fascinating phenomenon, but I suspect that the true nature of our modern era of celebrity experts and relaxed attitudes will only become clear through the lens of retrospect. In three or four decades' time, I expect that the students at some university faculty of Applied and Theoretical Sex Advice will be studying the Millennium Sexplosion with the same mirth, incredulity and horror that shakes us when we think of the masturbation scares of the Victorian era. What indeed will they think of us? Will they link our obsession with orgasms to our endless need to go shopping? Perhaps they will wonder why we bought so many manuals but seemed to have little time or energy for sex. Will they link that paradox with the way many of us buy celeb-chef cookbooks but rely on microwaves and eating meals out?

Already some commentators think our obsession with lovemaking has gone beyond all control (though haven't they always?) Sexual-health researchers from the London School of Hygiene and Tropical Medicine have warned in the *British Medical Journal* that, 'Until relatively recently, the imperative was for restraint and moderation in sexual matters; now it is for more and better sexual gratification. Celibacy is the new deviance. The irony is that we may be moving away from diversity towards greater uniformity. By encouraging women to look like *Playboy* centrefolds and men to seek priapic perfection, we may be furthering what has been termed the tyranny of genital sexuality.'

Genital tyranny. Could this be the next great sexual scare? Watch out.

SELECT BIBLIOGRAPHY

Aristotle's Works, Containing the Masterpiece.
   Directions for midwives, counsel and advice to
   childbearing women, with various useful
   remedies, London, *c.* 1860
Baden-Powell, Robert, *Rovering to Success*, Herbert
   Jenkins, 1922
Bell, Rudolph M., *How To Do It: guides to good*
   living for Renaissance Italians, Chicago
   University Press, 1999
Biale, David, *Eros and the Jews: from Biblical Israel*
   to contemporary America, Basic Books, 1995
Brandon, Ruth, *The New Women and the Old Men:*
   Love, sex and the woman question, Secker &
   Warburg, 1990
Burton, Richard, *The Ananga Ranga, Cosmopoli, For*
   the Kama Shastra Society of London and Benares,
   and for private circulation only, 1885
Burton, Richard and Arbuthnot, F.F. (trans.) *Kama*
   Sutra of Vatsyayana, ed. John Muirhead-Gould,
   Panther, 1963
Burton, Sir Richard, *The Perfumed Garden of the*
   Cheikh Nefzaoui: a manual of Arabian erotology
   (XVI Century) revised and corrected translation,

Cosmopoli: for the Kama Shastra Society of London and Benares, and for private circulation only, 1886

Bush, Michael, 'The Rise of the Sex Manual', *History Today*, 49:2, Feb. 1999

Bush, Michael *What Is Love? Richard Carlile's philosophy of sex*, Verso, 1998

Comfort, Alex (trans.) *Koka Shastra; being the Ratirahasya of Kokkoka and other medieval writings on love*, George Allen and Unwin, 1963

Comfort, Alex, *The Joy of Sex: a gourmet guide to lovemaking*, Fireside/Simon & Schuster, 1972

Chesler, Ellen, *Woman of Valor: Margaret Sanger and the birth-control movement in America*, Simon & Schuster, 1992

Cook, Hera, *The Long Sexual Revolution: English women, sex, and contraception 1800–1975*, Oxford University Press, 2004

Creese, Helen and Bellows, Laura, 'Erotic Literature in Nineteenth-century Bali', *Journal of Southeast Asian Studies*, 385, 33: 3, 2002

Darby, Robert, 'The Wroeites, William Chidley and the British Medical Association: bizarre sex cults in nineteenth-century Australia', seminar paper given to Australian National University History Department, 26 March 2004

D'Eath, Richard, *French Letters and English Overcoats*, Robson Books, 2000

DeRogatis, Amy, 'What Would Jesus Do? Sexuality and salvation in Protestant evangelical sex manuals, 1950s to the present', *Church History*, 74, 1: 97, 1 March 2005

Dutton, Geoffrey, *Kanga Creek: Havelock Ellis In Australia*, Picador, 1989

Ellis, A., *The Folklore of Sex*, Charles Boni, 1951

Ellis, Havelock, *Psychology of Sex: a manual for students*, William Heinemann Medical Books, 1933

Ellis, Havelock, *Sex and Marriage*, London: Williams and Norgate, 1951

Evans, B., *Freedom to Choose: the life and work of Dr Helena Wright, pioneer of contraception*, Bodley Head, 1982

Ferris, Paul, *Sex and the British: a twentieth-century history*, Michael Joseph, 1993

Frank, Thomas, *The Conquest of Cool*, University of Chicago Press, 1997

Grosskurth, Phyllis, *Havelock Ellis*, McClelland & Stewart, 1980

Hall, Lesley, *Hidden Anxieties: male sexuality 1900 to 1950*, Polity Press, 1991

Harper, Donald, *Early Chinese Medical Literature*, Columbia University Press, 1998

Laipson, Peter, '"Kiss Without Shame for She Desires It": sexual foreplay in medical advice literature, 1900–1925', *Journal of Social History*, March 1996

Laqueur, Thomas W., *Solitary Sex: a cultural history of masturbation*, Zone Books, 2003

Lewis, May J., *The Love Books of Ovid, being the Amores, Ars amatoria, Remedia Amoris and Medicamina Facei Famineae of Publius Ovidus Naso*, translated from the Latin, Rarity Press, 1930

Licht, H., *Sexual Life in Ancient Greece*, Kegan Paul, 2001

Lucretius, *On the Nature of the Universe*, translated by R.E. Latham, London, Penguin, 1951

McCarthy, Conor (ed.), Love, Sex and Marriage in the Middle Ages: a sourcebook, London and New York: Routledge, 2004

Melody, M.E. and Peterson, Linda M., *Teaching America about Sex: marriage guides and sex manuals from the late Victorians to Dr Ruth*, New York University Press, 1999

Navas, Carmen Caballero (ed. and trans.), *The Book of Women's Love and Jewish Medieval Medical Literature on Women*, Kegan Paul, 2004

Petersen, James R., 'A Brief History of Sex Tricks: what sex manuals tell us about ourselves', *Playboy*, 1 September 1996

Porter, Roy and Hall, Lesley, *The Facts of Life: the creation of sexual knowledge in Britain, 1650–1950*, Yale University Press, 1995

Porter, Roy and Teich, Mikulas (eds), *Sexual Knowledge, Sexual Science: the history of attitudes towards sexuality*, Cambridge University Press, 1994

Rashkow, Ilona N., *Taboo or not Taboo; sexuality and family in the Hebrew Bible*, Fortress Press, 2000

Rusbridger, Alan, *A Concise History of the Sex Manual 1886–1986*, Faber and Faber, 1986

Smithers, Leonard C. and Burton, Richard, *Priapeia sive diversorum poetarum in Priapum lusus, or sportive epigrams on Priapus by divers poets in English verse and prose translation*, 1890

Stall, Sylvanus, *What a Young Boy Ought to Know*, William Briggs, 1905

Stengers Jean and Van Neck, Anne *Masturbation: the history of a great terror*, Palgrave/St. Martins, 2001

Stolberg, Michael, 'Self-Pollution, Moral Reform, and the Venereal Trade: notes on the sources and historical context of *Onania* (1716)', *Journal of the History of Sexuality*, 9, 1–2: 37–61, January/April 2000

Stopes, Marie Carmichael, *Married Love: a new contribution to the solution of sex difficulties*, Cambridge University Press, 1923 (12th edition)

Van de Velde, Theodoor Hendrik, *Ideal Marriage*, Random House, 1930

Van Gulik, R.H. and Goldin, P.R., *Sexual Life in Ancient China: a preliminary survey of Chinese sex and society from 1500 BC till AD 1644*, Brill Academic Publishers, 2003

Van Gulik, R.H., *Erotic Colour Prints of the Ming Period, with an Essay on Chinese Sex Life from the Han to the Ching Dynasty, 206 BC–AD 1644 (Sinica Leidensia)*, Brill Academic Publishers, 2004

Venette, Nicholas, *Conjugal Love; or the pleasures of the marriage bed considered in several lectures on human generation. From the French of Venette, an eminent surgeon and member of the Royal Academy of Paris*, 12th edn, first published 1703

Walters, Ronald G (ed.), *Primers for Prudery: sexual advice to Victorian America*, Johns Hopkins University Press, 2000

Weininger, Otto, *Sex and Character*, 14th ed, Wilhelm Braumiller, 1913

Wieringa, Edwin P., 'A Javanese Handbook for Would-be Husbands: the Serat candraning wanita', *Journal of Southeast Asian Studies*, 431, 33: 3, 2002

Wright, Thomas, *The Life of Sir Richard Burton*, Burt Franklin, 1968

INDEX